Dot Journaling

A PRACTICAL GUIDE

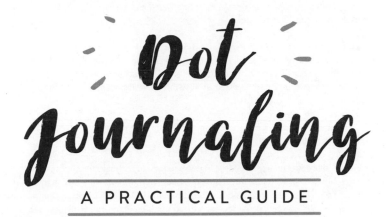

Dot Journaling

A PRACTICAL GUIDE

How to Start and Keep the

PLANNER, TO-DO LIST, and DIARY

That'll Actually Help You

Get Your Life Together

RACHEL WILKERSON MILLER

THE EXPERIMENT

NEW YORK

The Experiment, LLC, 220 East 23rd Street, Suite 301, New York, NY 10010-4674
theexperimentpublishing.com

The Experiment's books are available at special discounts when purchased in bulk for premiums and sales promotions as well as for fund-raising or educational use. For details, contact us at info@theexperimentpublishing.com.

Library of Congress Cataloging-in-Publication Data

Names: Miller, Rachel Wilkerson, author.
Title: Dot journaling--a practical guide : how to start and keep the planner,
   to-do list, and diary that'll actually help you get your life together /
   Rachel Wilkerson Miller.
Description: New York, NY : The Experiment, LLC, [2017] | Includes
   bibliographical references.
Identifiers: LCCN 2017012042 | ISBN 9781615194070 (pbk.)
Subjects: LCSH: Time management. | Diaries--Authorship. | Planning. |
   Appointment books.
Classification: LCC BF637.T5 M55 2017 | DDC 650.1/1--dc23
LC record available at https://lccn.loc.gov/2017012042

ISBN 978-1-61519-407-0
Ebook ISBN 978-1-61519-427-8

Cover and text design by Sarah Smith
Photography and prop styling by Sarah Smith
Author photograph by Katherine O'Brien

Manufactured in China
Distributed by Workman Publishing Company, Inc.
Distributed simultaneously in Canada by Thomas Allen & Son Ltd.

First printing July 2017
10 9 8 7 6 5 4 3 2 1

CONTENTS

"

A wish to record the passing events of my life, which, even if quite unimportant to others, naturally possess great interest to myself, and of which it will be pleasant to have some remembrance, has induced me to commence this journal. I feel that keeping a diary will be a pleasant and profitable employment of my leisure hours, and will afford me much pleasure in after years, by recalling to my mind the memories of other days, thoughts of much-loved friends from whom I may be separated, with whom I now pass many happy hours, in taking delightful walks, and holding "sweet converse"; the interesting books that I read; and the different people, places and things that I am permitted to see. Besides this, it will doubtless enable me to judge correctly of the growth and improvement of my mind from year to year.

— CHARLOTTE FORTEN GRIMKÉ
in her diary, May 1854

————

Jesus, I am graduating in four days a VIRGIN!!!
— ME in my diary, May 29, 2003

"

INTRO

started my first diary when I was nine years old and in fourth grade. Onward through middle school, high school, college, and my early twenties, I wrote almost every single day, filling notebook after notebook with my thoughts and observations. (And my crushes. *So* many crushes.) I also used a physical planner and wrote out my to-do list every single day, long after apps and websites made both unnecessary.

But in the second half of my twenties, my diary writing slowed down, then ground to a halt. Part of this happened because I was writing as my full-time job, plus keeping a blog. But I was also sharing my thoughts with my friends via texts, instant messages, and emails all day, and I didn't feel like rewriting everything in a notebook at night. And though I still wrote out to-do lists every day in a steno pad, it wasn't a habit that I did with a sense of intention, or that gave me any real sense of joy.

So, this is where I was in my journaling ~journey~ when I came to dot journaling a couple years ago. I first read about something called a "Bullet Journal" on my friend Jessica's blog in December 2015, and was intrigued. Initially, I assumed it was some sort of new diary or planner to buy—and I thought, *Great, I love buying new things!* But when I went to the official website run by its creator, Ryder Carroll, I just got confused. Not only was it *not* something to buy, I couldn't understand what, exactly, it was. When I heard "journal," I thought "diary," but this seemed like it was a ... to-do list? And also a ... calendar? Or ... something? There were bullet points involved, and also a lot of words and phrases that I didn't recognize, along with photos of incredibly simple journal pages that seemed to have very little in common with the elaborate, creative, beautiful pages I was seeing on Instagram—pages that were also, somehow (apparently?), from Bullet Journals. It seemed like a lot of people were using dot-grid journals to do ... whatever it was they were doing, but that type of paper didn't appear to be a requirement. I couldn't figure out what the rules were, or exactly what the point was, either. Eventually, I gave up.

But after asking around and discovering that my friends had *also* been hearing about this new type of journal and *also* couldn't understand what it was, I became determined to figure it out. Turns out, Bullet Journaling is an incredibly simple concept that is *remarkably* difficult to explain, in part because "you do you" is such a major aspect of it—meaning everyone does it a little differently, and there are no real rules. And, over time, the Internet has transformed the basic idea—using simple symbols and dot-grid journals to record the things that matter most—into what I've come to think of as "dot journaling" ... aka, a creative, colorful, robust, and—listen, take this with a large grain of salt—Pinteresty version of the original concept.

I started dot journaling on January 1, 2016, and I quickly fell in love. It was exactly what I hadn't realized I needed: a single notebook that incorporated my to-do lists, helped me stay organized, served as a fun creative outlet, and led me back to my roots as a diarist—I was thrilled to discover that I had no problem writing in it every single day. And in this book, I'll show you how to get started dot journaling, and how to make it a habit (or an addiction?) for you, too.

SO WHAT EXACTLY IS A DOT JOURNAL?

A dot journal is a system for writing down *all* the things that you want to remember in a single notebook: things that you want or need to do, things you've already done, and your thoughts/observations—from every aspect of your life (work, home, relationships, hobbies, etc.). When you're writing in your journal (which can be any notebook you like), you'll jot everything down quickly using short words/phrases (instead of writing in full sentences), and you'll mark each item with one of a handful of simple symbols—hint: The main one is a *dot*, hence the name—so you can easily categorize the information and find it later. Along with these symbols, you'll also utilize a few very basic methods of organization: dates, page numbers, titles, topics/categories, and an index.

Dot journaling is an amazing way of recording everything that matters to you and keeping your life together both figuratively and literally.

t. 04.09.17

- follow up on Ali's email
- ^ submit docs for review
- · sign off on brochure design
- ☑ 7 a.m. workout class
- ✗ call about couch delivery
- ＞ check timesheets
- ☒ 5:30 p.m. Project Beta Fish info session
- ☒ 7 p.m. class

notes

- It was SO dark this morning & my bed was SO cozy and all I wanted to do was stay there snuggling with Sam.
- Trekked all the way to my hot yoga class... only to realize I had mixed up my days and the class wasn't until 8:30. Did 30 minutes of cardio and a 20-minute yoga podcast instead
- Showered & got ready at the gym and got in to work a little early, which was nice. Most people get in at 10, but I like being part of the early morning crew
- Found out today that the couch is backordered AGAIN. How?!
- Back was sore again today... I need to start setting reminders to get up & move throughout the day. I feel like my spine is turning to mush.

OK, still with me? Sort of? Wonderful.

We begin with a fresh notebook. This notebook can have blank pages, lined pages, graph paper pages, or dot-grid pages; *the most important thing is that it doesn't have any sort of pre-printed text telling you what to write and where to write it*—so no preprinted dates, no weekly calendar, no hourly agenda, no header that reads "Write Your To-Do List Here" with numbered lines below it, etc. (Page numbers, however, are fine.)

The problem with predesigned journals and planners is that they can't accurately predict your needs, or fully accommodate them. They don't know how big your handwriting is, or how much space you'll need to write a to-do list or a diary entry each day. *You* don't even know how much space you'll need each day. Maybe you need four lines! Maybe you need four *pages*! Maybe—probably—it depends on the day. The reason dot journaling is so appealing is because it gives you a structure to organize your thoughts, but you get to decide exactly how you want this planner/journal/notebook *thing* to work and look. And instead of trying to figure everything out in advance (which would be impossible), you just set up the first few pages, and then you set up more pages as you go along, wherever you are in the notebook.

Nothing to see
here, folks!

Q. IS A DOT JOURNAL A TO-DO LIST OR A PLANNER OR A DIARY? A. *YES.*

This was my main question before I started dot journaling, and I was very annoyed when people told me it was all of these things. But it *is* all of these things!

Planners and to-do lists typically focus on what you're going to do, and diaries tend to focus on the things you've already done. But combining *all* of these things gives us a complete picture of who we are. Before I started dot journaling, I could not fathom keeping my work tasks, my personal to-do list, and my diary in the same place. (Even when I first started, I told myself I was only going to use my dot journal as a personal journal, not for anything work-related; this approach lasted, like, two weeks.) But the journaling system I use makes it easy to organize the different parts of your life in a single notebook in a way that makes sense. And, more important, I can now understand *why* it makes sense to do it that way.

When I look back at my old diaries, I'm always amazed by how much I left out of them. I wrote a lot about boys, and far less about school, my friends, books I was reading, money, goals I was working toward, or simply what my daily routine was like. My to-do lists may have contained some of that information, but I didn't bother to hang on to them because I didn't think they were important. But I've since realized that our tasks, habits, and routines actually reveal a lot about what we prioritize, what we aspire to, and who we are. Dot journaling helps you record *all* of the things that are going on in your life, and makes it easy to keep track of everything you want to do in the future.

Dot journaling is good for . . .

- People who like pen and paper to-do lists
- People who have a million to-do lists floating around
- People who are really into setting goals
- People who like stationery, journaling, scrapbooking, beautiful pens, etc.
- People who really love planners
- People who really *want* to love planners, or who want to be more organized
- People who would really like to keep a journal/diary but are having trouble sticking with the habit.

But! None of these are requirements for enjoying dot journaling. Ultimately, dot journaling (and this book) is for nice people who want to write sh*t down and get sh*t done.

March 01, 2017

- ☓ pay rent
- ☓ pay student loan payment
- ☒ 2:30 p.m. design meeting
- · work out
- › buy dog food
- ∧ work on HOB proposal
- · request vacation time
- · sign up for training session

ABOUT THIS BOOK

This book will explain exactly what dot journaling is, show you examples of popular ways people use the system, give you ideas for setting up your dot journal, answer the most common questions new journalers have, and provide tips for fitting dot journaling into your life. Whether you're totally new to the concept, or have been dot journaling for a while, this book is for you.

One of the best aspects of dot journaling—and a huge reason for its popularity—is how *adaptable* it is. Once you grasp the basic concept, the ways you can use the system are truly endless. And on that note, everything in this book should be taken as a friendly suggestion, *not* a requirement; the "rules" are really just recommendations, and you should feel free to use your journal in a way that makes sense for *you*.

There are as many styles of dot journals as there are dot journalers. Many enthusiasts put a lot of time into making their pages look gorgeous, and treat dot journaling like a creative outlet or hobby. But there are far, far more people who take a simple/minimalist/messy approach, and that's fine, too. (Seriously, at least once a week, someone starts a "Shout out to everyone with awful handwriting whose journal doesn't look Pinterest-perfect!" thread in the journaling Facebook group I'm in, and it always gets tons of positive responses.)

My goal was to create dot journal layouts for this book that are simple enough that they'll spark creativity, and pretty enough that you'll enjoy looking at them. But you should keep in mind that the journal pages you will see throughout this book are *not real*. They contain fictional scenarios, tasks, and people, and were made to look good in photos. I wrote slowly so my handwriting would look nice. If I made mistakes when I was working on them, I started over, because making them look perfect is *literally my job*. I promise, my actual journal contains considerably more correction tape, crooked lines, and curse words. And yours probably will, too.

Throughout this book, I'll use the words *journal* and *note-book* interchangeably to refer to the physical book itself. I'll also shorten *dot journal* to *journal*. *Dot grid* and *dot-grid journal* are what I call a notebook with paper that's similar to graph paper but that is marked with dots instead of lines. When I say *calendar* and *planner*, I mean the book that typically comes with predesigned pages, where people traditionally keep track of events that have a specific date/time and the tasks that they need to get done in a given day. I use both *spread* and *layout* when discussing ways of organizing information on the pages of your dot journal. And when I say *diary*, I'm referring to the physical notebook and the type of writing where you record daily interactions and experiences in first person, often with additional reflection. (You know, the kind of thing that could start "Dear Diary. . . .")

"WHY BOTHER?"

At first glance, dot journaling can seem complicated, and you might not see the point of it. But I'd like to make the case for why you should bother. (Or, at least, why *I* bother.)

First, dot journaling is an excellent way to be more organized. Aside from keeping me gainfully employed, being organized is one way I practice self-care. Because, look: Not having
your life together—forgetting to do important tasks, losing
critical documents and information, running late all the time,
worrying about money—isn't exactly fun. It's *stressful*. So
being organized is one way to remove unnecessary anxiety
from your life. Tracking your day-to-day life also makes it easier to understand exactly what makes you happy and healthy
(and what makes you *un*happy and *un*healthy), achieve your
goals, and live your best life.

In addition to serving my own needs, I look at being organized as a gift to other people. The older I get, the more I
understand that my personal decisions and my overall mood
have a major effect on those around me. And when I don't do
important things—whether that's paying a bill or preparing
for a meeting or showing up on time or going to the doctor—it
matters. So being organized is a way of saying to the people I
care about, "I value your time, I recognize that we are in this
together, and I want to be at my best for you."

Second, dot journaling (like all journaling/diary keeping) is
a way of better understanding who you are, and making sense of
the world around you. A dot journal makes it easier to answer
important questions—both "What time is that appointment?"
and "Did I send that tax form?" and also "Do I maybe have
an unhealthy relationship with [food/a love interest/*Grey's
Anatomy*]?" In a busy world filled with so much noise and no
shortage of cynicism, having a small space that is yours and
yours alone, where you can candidly share your most private
moments and deepest (or shallowest!) thoughts without fear

of judgment, is beautiful and special. Our journals are often the first place where we can say these things; sometimes, they are the *only* place where we can say these things.

Writing about yourself and your life—even just brief notes!—is a huge privilege, and that writing can be incredibly liberating. Writing in a diary is, at its core, a declaration that your voice matters. If you're one of the many people who is told the opposite by society—told that you should be quieter, that expressing your own needs makes you selfish or "crazy," that you mostly exist to take care of other people—then choosing to speak your truth can be a powerful act. It's a way of saying, "I'm more than a supporting character in someone else's narrative; *I* am the hero of this story, and what I do, say, think, and feel has value." And finding your voice in private makes it much easier to find your voice in public.

So maybe dot journaling will help you answer the big, scary questions about who you are and what you want out of life. Or maybe it'll just help you pay your cable bill on time. Either way, I think it's pretty worth it.

THREE TIPS FOR GETTING STARTED

1. **Keep it simple, especially at first.** There are so many amazing possibilities for dot journaling, and it can be tempting to go all-in with complicated, colorful layouts immediately. But focusing too much on how your journal looks can make you more likely to get overwhelmed and ultimately give up. When I started my first dot journal, I forced myself to keep it super simple so that I'd actually do it. After a month, once I was sure that the habit was going to stick, I felt more confident adding in some color. After about six weeks, I started doing more complex weekly spreads. But if I'd done everything at once, I'm not sure I would have stuck with it.

2. **Do a little preplanning.** If the sight of a blank notebook fills you with both intense joy and overwhelming anxiety, and if you hate making mistakes in pen, I recommend that after reading this book, you sit down with a couple of sheets of scrap paper and write out the spreads you want to try on each of the first few

pages of your journal, before you actually start setting it up. (You could also use sticky notes to designate the content you're envisioning for each page.) On the other hand, don't try to plan the entire journal before you get started—it's basically impossible, especially at the beginning. Which leads me to . . .

3. Don't overthink it! When you're setting up your first dot journal, it's easy to feel like you need to make decisions that you can live with *forever*. But that's not the case at all. Dot journaling is all about flexibility, and most people who do it reevaluate their spreads every month (or every week) to decide what's working and what's not. Once you give yourself permission to change your approach whenever you feel like it, and accept that your dot journal isn't going to be perfect—and that the way it looks on day 1 is likely not the way it will look on day 60—it's *much* easier to get started (and to keep going).

CHAPTER 1

The Basics

Hearing people talk about dot journaling can feel a bit like listening to people speak a foreign language. *OK, but what the heck is a "future spread"?* you think as you scroll through photos on Instagram of beautiful hand-drawn calendars filled with strange symbols that you don't recognize. *Why does she keep talking about "dailies" as though I know what that means?* you wonder about your friend who recently became obsessed with dot journaling and who is now trying to get you to do the same. And, look, I get it. The first time I read about this system, I gave up after two minutes because I was so confused and overwhelmed by the terminology. So let's kick things off with a vocabulary lesson.

Dot journaling: a method of planning, journaling, and note-taking that involves writing quick, short phrases or sentences and marking them with simple symbols so you can easily categorize and track them. When you're writing in your dot journal, the idea is to keep each item super brief, even if you're dealing with something really major and dramatic. (Keeping it brief means you'll probably be more likely to actually write things down. But! If you want, you can expand on these items on the next page in full sentences like you would in a typical diary.) The items you'll jot down in your dot journal mostly fall into three categories: tasks, events, and notes.

Tasks: things you need to do or have already done

Events: things that are going to happen, and things that already have

Notes: thoughts, observations, and basically everything that is neither a task nor an event

Dot: the main symbol you'll use when writing items in your dot journal; it signifies "this is a task that you need to complete"

Spread: the way information is organized on a page (or across multiple pages) in your dot journal; used interchangeably with "layout." Spreads can be complicated/artistic/fancy, or they can just be plain, old-fashioned lists. Regardless, your spreads will likely be defined by a specific time frame (like "this week") or by a specific topic ("books I want to read"); they can also be a little bit of both ("reading I need to do this week").

Title: the word/phrase you write somewhere on a spread—most likely at the top—that says what the spread is (like "March 25, 2017" or "My Enemies"). May also be referred to as a "header."

Future spread: a year-at-a-glance calendar where you can put events, goals, and long-term things you need to do

Monthly spread: a monthly calendar + things you need to do that month + things you forgot to do last month

Weekly spread (aka "weeklies"): a weekly calendar + things you need to do that week + things you forgot to do last week

Daily spread (aka "dailies"): the things you did and/or need to do today, plus other observations

Habit trackers: spreads where you enter activities you do regularly. You can track habits at the yearly, weekly, monthly, or daily level, or by category, or (you guessed it!) a little bit of Column A and a little bit of Column B.

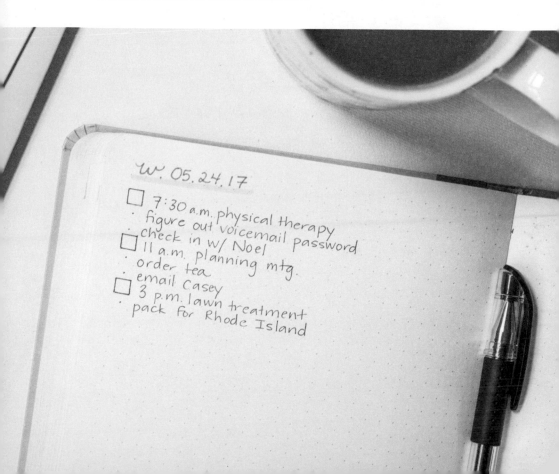

Dot journaling is essentially just creating spreads and then adding information to them as appropriate. When you set up your first dot journal, you'll (most likely) create a yearly spread and a monthly spread (for whatever month it is when you're starting). But rather than setting up, say, every daily page for the entire month at once and trying to estimate how much space you'll need for each day in advance, you'll just create each daily spread the day of. You can set up spreads tied to particular topics or categories when you first start your dot

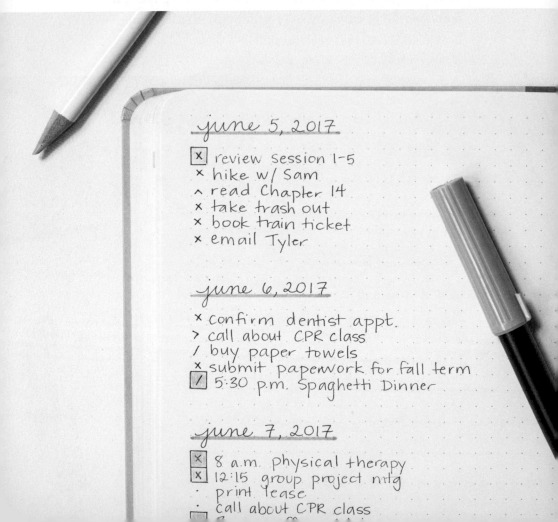

journal, or you can also create them anytime you feel like it, wherever you are in the journal.

So, let's imagine you've been dot journaling for a little while, and that you woke up today and realized that you'd very much like to make a list of everything you want to do on a trip you've just started planning. Great! So you'd go to the next page in your dot journal and write "Vermont Trip" at the top (that's your title), and then you'd just start writing ideas down below that! Now, you may be thinking, *Here? On page twenty-seven? Randomly sandwiched between a Tuesday page and a Wednesday page? In a notebook owned by me, a perfectionist who likes everything just so?* And the answer is: Yes! Right there! On page twenty-seven, in *your* notebook! This is what separates a dot journal from a preprinted planner. That off-the-shelf, one-size-fits-all planner doesn't know that you'll need a space for a travel list on this exact page. But your dot journal is like, "HELLO, I WELCOME YOUR EVERY SPONTANEOUS THOUGHT! JUST WRITE WHAT YOU NEED TO WRITE WHEREVER YOU ARE IN THE NOTEBOOK AND I WILL MAKE IT EASY FOR YOU TO FIND THE INFORMATION LATER!" *"How* will it be easy to find the information later?" you ask. Well, that brings us to . . .

THE INDEX

The index is typically the first page you'll set up in your dot journal; like a traditional book index, it's a list of topics and the page numbers on which they appear. So every time you write about something important that you'll likely want to reference later, you'll flip to your index and write the topic and the corresponding page number there.

Now, you may be thinking, *Wait—did you say "page numbers"?* I sure did! Another hallmark of a dot journal is that *every page in your notebook gets a number.* If your journal doesn't have prenumbered pages (which is highly likely), you can just number them yourself. You *could* number every single page before you start, but if you're lazy like I am, you can do like I do and just number about twenty pages at a time.

Anyway, when you first start your dot journal, there probably won't be much to put in the index—you'll go back to the index and add in the topics and the page numbers as you start using the journal. I usually give myself two or three pages for my index, just to be on the safe side. (By the way, there's no rule that says the index has to be at the beginning; my friend Nicole puts her index at the back of her dot journal. Follow your heart, folks.)

You don't have to put *everything* in your index, but it's worthwhile to add lists, events, spreads, and ideas you know you will probably want to reference later. And the items in your index can be as specific or as general as you like. For example, you can create a single entry, "Travel," and then write all travel-related page numbers there, *or* you can list specific travel topics separately (like "Texas trip" and "Vermont vacation") in your index. These days, I try not to get *too* granular—after a few months, I realized that recording *every* mention of my closest friends wasn't terribly useful or efficient. On the other hand, I recently started adding an entry for each week to my index, and have found that to be helpful. My advice is to play with different options and adjust as necessary as you go.

While I'd never considered putting an index in a diary or notebook before I started dot journaling, I've found that it's

index

a pretty brilliant idea. You'll likely find yourself creating new, important pages at random spots throughout your journal, and it's great to know *exactly* where each one is. It may seem like a hassle to keep updating the index, but in a few months, when you're flipping through your journal trying to find something important that you could *swear* you wrote down—and when your brain keeps telling you "Just type it into the 'search' box!" and you realize that computers have ruined our damn minds—you will be glad you have an index.

THE PETTIEST INDEX

Mrs. Betsey Fremantle (née Wynne) kept diaries throughout her life in the eighteenth and nineteenth centuries, diaries that were later published by her great-granddaughter Anne Fremantle. The index to volume I, prepared by Anne, contains the following entry:

> dislikes Bombelles family, 119, 157, 164, 165, 170, 174, 175, 177-9, 183, 184, 186, 187, 190, 191, 202, 207, 208, 211, 213, 220, 224, 225, 229, 230, 231, 235, 236, 254, 260, 261, 271

I'm not saying you should create an index entry for every time you trash-talk someone or something . . . but I'm not saying you *shouldn't* do that, either.

THE SYMBOLS

The symbols are one of the core aspects of what makes a dot journal, well, a dot journal. Here are the symbols that I've come to find most useful and that you'll see throughout this book.

Write a **dot** next to things that you need to do.

Draw an **x** over the dot to mark to-dos that are complete.

Write the **less-than symbol (<)** over the dot to show that a task has been scheduled, or write the **greater-than symbol (>)** over it to show that the task has been migrated—aka you didn't finish it today/this week/this month, so you moved it to another day's/week's/month's list. You can migrate the same item over and over and over again until you finally complete it (or until you finally say, "Wow, this is never going to

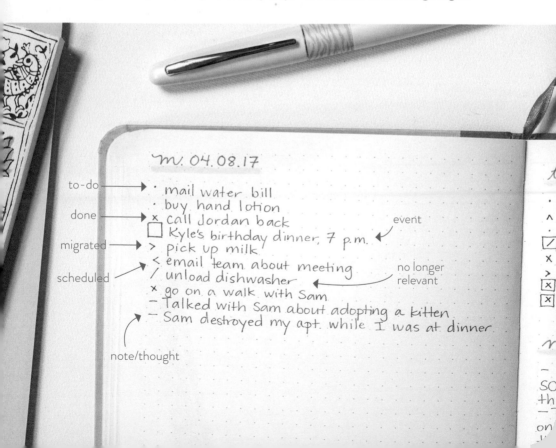

happen," and let it go). Not that I'd know anything about that. P.S. Notice how you can easily turn either of these symbols into an **x** once the task is complete.

Add a **caret (^)** over the dot when you've started a task. (Because even if you don't finish it, it's nice to feel like you accomplished *something*.)

Use a **dash** for quick thoughts, notes, observations, or smaller events.

Draw an **open box** to mark big events (appointments, birthdays, meetings, anniversaries, etc.).

Put a **slash** through any items that are no longer relevant.

I also write the **x** and other symbols inside the event box when appropriate. (For example, if an event gets rescheduled, I draw the migration symbol in the box. If the event is canceled, I put a slash in the box.) And when writing about big moments in my diary section, I use the event box, and then color the box in with one of three markers, depending on what kind of event it was.

If these symbols don't speak to you, below are some other popular symbol sets that might inspire you. Regardless of the exact symbols you use, it can be helpful to write them all down in a key, which I usually put on the last page of my dot journal.

"UM, A TO-DO LIST WHERE YOU DON'T CROSS THINGS OUT? BUT THAT'S THE BEST PART OF A TO-DO LIST!"

Listen, I hear you. I'm the kind of person who adds things to her to-do list just so she can cross them off, so this was one of my immediate concerns when I first saw these symbols in other people's journals. But after a few weeks of using the system as designed, I actually came to prefer the dot and x approach.

First, it's helpful to be able to go back and read an entire item, even if you've completed it. Drawing a line through an entire event, or an item that has been scheduled, doesn't feel quite right. And *not* drawing lines through tasks makes the entire notebook look cleaner, which I appreciate. Additionally, as I mentioned earlier, the x works nicely in conjunction with the other symbols.

Once I unclutched my pearls and made the switch, I realized that writing an x over a dot is still pretty darn satisfying. (I definitely still add completed tasks to my list just to be able to do that!) So give these other symbols a try and see what you think. If, after trying them, you find that drawing a line through to-dos is an itch you absolutely have to scratch, then by all means, don't let me stop you! But my guess is you won't miss it as much as you think you will.

CHOOSING A NOTEBOOK

You can dot journal in *any* notebook that you like—you're not required to buy a specific brand, size, or style. Here are a few tips to keep in mind when selecting your notebook:

- Get a notebook that's big enough that you can write a lot in it—so, something with a good number of pages (think:

150 to 250), and with pages that are big enough that you won't fill them up with just a couple of sentences (so, probably something larger than pocket-size). Most dot journalers opt for something around five inches wide by eight inches tall.

- Don't get a notebook that's so big or heavy that you won't want to carry it around with you. You don't need to have it with you *all* the time, but "Will this fit in my regular purse/bag?" is a good question to ask.

- Choose something sturdy. While notebooks with a thin cardboard cover are typically lighter and cheaper than their hardcover counterparts, they can also end up very battered, very quickly.

- You can dot journal in a notebook with blank pages, lined pages, or some kind of graph paper; it's really a matter of personal preference. A lot of journalers, myself included, use dot-grid notebooks. I'd never used (or even *seen*) this kind of paper before I started dot journaling, and now I can't imagine using anything else. Blank pages stress me out (Am I writing in a straight line? No, of course I'm not!), and lined pages don't offer as much flexibility for layouts and text size as dot-grid pages do. Plus, the dots are typically *very* faint, so the book actually looks blank from far away—which means that people who glance at your journal in passing will think you are secretly a witch, because how else would you be able to write such perfectly even rows of text on blank pages?

- Don't stress too much about your journal choice. If you don't like the notebook you start with, you can switch to one you like better whenever you feel like it. You may even want to use an inexpensive notebook at first, and then upgrade to one of the pricier ones after you have a better idea of what you like and need.

"AIN'T NOBODY GOT TIME FOR THAT!"

This is a lot of people's first reaction upon learning about dot journaling, especially on the Internet, and while I understand it, it's not exactly accurate. A lot of people have time for it. Or, more accurately, a lot of people *make* time for it.

Dot journaling takes up as much or as little time as you want it to. The initial setup takes less than an hour, and I tend to write in mine for ten to thirty minutes each night. Like most things, I've found that once I get going, I often end up doing more than I expected to, but sometimes I just write for five minutes and call it a night. Beyond that, I spend about ten or fifteen minutes every Sunday setting up my new weekly spread, and about thirty minutes each month creating new pages for the upcoming month.

Because I enjoy doing it, working on my dot journal never feels like it's taking *that* much time. And because it's time I'd probably otherwise waste looking at dumb stuff on the Internet, it's not *really* time I miss. Writing about my day is a lovely way to unplug and unwind before bed, so I look at it as time well spent—especially when I consider that taking five to ten minutes to make a to-do list every day means I'm less likely to waste an hour being stressed out or running unnecessary errands because I forgot something important.

There are definitely people who spend more time on their dot journals; they enjoy looking for ideas and inspiration, building relationships with other dot journalers, creating beautiful new layouts, and discussing important topics like where to buy the perfect sticky notes, or what the best brand of black gel pen is. Many of them are people who were looking for a creative outlet, and their dot journal became that. But that approach isn't a requirement. And those extras never need to interfere with our core reasons for dot journaling: organization, self-reflection, self-improvement, and getting stuff done.

The majority of dot journalers I know are moms, students, people who work outside the home, or all of the above. They know that what they get out of dot journaling is worth the time they put in—whether that's five minutes or an hour a day. Trudelle Thomas, PhD, a professor and researcher at Xavier University in Cincinnati, Ohio, who conducted in-depth interviews with fifteen ordinary people who have kept diaries consistently for at least five years, found this to be the case with her research subjects, writing:

> *I was struck by how busy they were. Many were involved in demanding careers, several were raising young children, and most had commitments to social activism, church work, or artistic pursuits as well. Yet all had managed to weave the diary into their lives for substantial lengths of time. . . . Evidently the practice of keeping a diary had great value for them.*

So if you find that dot journaling adds value to your life, you'll find time for it. And, look: If you have the time to write "Who has that kind of time?" on things you see on the Internet, the answer is probably . . . you. *You have the time, angry Internet commenter.*

"

The impulse to write things down is a peculiarly
compulsive one, inexplicable to those who do not share
it, useful only accidentally, only secondarily, in the way
that any compulsion tries to justify itself. . . . Keepers of
private notebooks are a different breed altogether, lonely
and resistant rearrangers of things, anxious malcontents,
children afflicted apparently at birth with some
presentiment of loss.

—JOAN DIDION

"

CHAPTER 2

Yearly Spreads

Once you've set up your index, you'll devote a few pages to the year ahead. These pages are what's known as your "future spread," which is just fancy journal speak for "calendar." The future spread is for big events, deadlines, birthdays, appointments, and long-term planning, and you'll use the symbols described in the last chapter to mark the different items. (If you're starting your dot journal midyear, you can either do future planning for just the remaining months in the year, or you can also include the previous months, and write in the big events that have already happened.)

When you're first setting up your journal, you don't need to fill out these spreads entirely. Create the layouts and add whatever items you can think of now, and then update them as time goes on.

Here are some ideas for what your yearly spreads could look like.

Simple date list

This six-page layout is straightforward and easy to create—no artistic skills required! Split the page into two columns, and then write all the days in the month down the left side of each column. This a good spread if you don't expect to have many events to add for each date, and if your handwriting is on the smaller side.

02

W 1
T 2
F 3
S 4
S 5
M 6
T 7
W 8
T 9 ☐ Jules & Quinn visit
F 10 ☐ Jules & Quinn visit
S 11 ☐ Jules & Quinn visit
S 12 ☐ Jules & Quinn visit

M 13
T 14
W 15
T 16
F 17
S 18
S 19 ☐ Jordan birthday
M 20 ☐ Presidents Day

T 21
W 22
T 23
F 24
S 25
S 26
M 27
T 28

03

W 1
T 2 · proposal draft due
F 3
S 4
S 5
M 6
T 7
W 8
T 9
F 10 ☐ Alex birthday
S 11
S 12
M 13 · proposal draft → Noel
T 14
W 15
T 16
F 17 · submit proposal
S 18
S 19
M 20
T 21
W 22
T 23 ☐ Austin trip
F 24 ☐ Austin trip
S 25 ☐ Austin trip
S 26 ☐ Austin trip
M 27
T 28
W 29
T 30
F 31

04

S 1
S 2
M 3
T 4
W 5
T 6
F 7
S 8 ☐ Kyle birthday
S 9
M 10
T 11
W 12 ☐ HOB Summit
T 13 ☐ HOB Summit
F 14 ☐ HOB Summit
S 15
S 16
M 17
T 18
W 19
T 20
F 21
S 22
S 23
M 24 ☐ house-sit
T 25 ☐ house-sit
W 26 ☐ house-sit
T 27 ☐ house-sit
F 28 ☐ house-sit
S 29
S 30

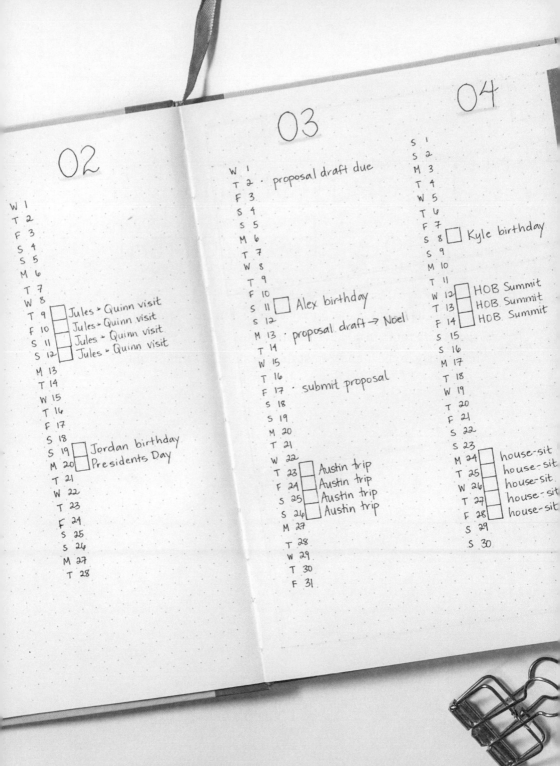

Three months per page—horizontal

This is the layout I used for my very first future spread; it gives you more room to add events and notes because you don't list every day in the month—just the ones that are important.

JAN.

- ☐ 01/02: office closed
- ☐ 01/16 MLK Day

MAR.

- ☐ 03/11: Alex's birthday
- ☐ 03/23-03/26: trip to Austin

MAY

- book hotel for Taylor + Tyler's wedding
- get passport photos taken

Three months per page—vertical

This four-page spread combines the features I like best from the first two layouts; it has vertical columns (with optional mini calendars), but it doesn't list every single day in the month.

07

S	M	T	W	T	F	S
						1
2	3	4	5	6	7	8
9	10	11	12	13	14	15
16	17	18	19	20	21	22
23	24	25	26	27	28	29
30	31					

☐ 6/30-7/9: Rhode Island trip
☐ 7/13: dr. appt.
☐ 7/25: eye doctor

08

S			W	T	F	S
				2	3	4
6	7	8	9	10	11	
13	14	15	16	17	18	
20	21	22	23	24	25	
27	28	29	30	31		

☐ 8/4-8/7: Vermont
☐ 8/16: neig meetin
· make
Homec

Four months per page

A four-square grid is one of my favorite ways to design pages in my dot journal. It's another one that's so *easy*—all you need is a ruler and a pen.

September

- [ ] 09/04: Labor Day

October

- [ ] 10/07: Chris + Skylar's wedding
- [ ] 10/14: Homecoming

November

- [ ] 11/23: Thanksgiving

December

- [ ] 12/06: Austin's bday
- [ ] 12/07- 12/10: Jules visit

Six months per page

This spread makes it possible to see the entire year without having to flip pages, which I appreciate. Since it only takes up two pages, it's good for people who don't want to devote too much space to their future spread.

JAN.

☐ 01/02: office closed
☐ 01/13: application due
☐ 01/16: MLK Day

MAY

☐ 05/03: Tracy bday
· book hotel for Tay and Tyler's weddin
· get passport photos taken

SEP.

☐ 09/04: Labor Da

EB.

- ☐ 02/09-02/12: Jules + Quinn visit
- ☐ 02/19: Jordan bday
- ☐ 02/20: Presidents Day

MAR.

- · 03/13: submit proposal draft to Noel
- ☐ 03/11: Alex birthday
- · 03/17: submit final proposal
- ☐ 03/23-03/26: Austin trip

APR.

- ☐ 04/08: Kyle
- ☐ 04/12-04/14: Summit
- ☐ 04/24-04/28 for Lee

JUN.

- · submit passport application
- ☐ 06/17: Taylor + Tyler's wedding

JUL.

- ☐ 06/30-07/09: Rhode Island vacation

AUG.

- ☐ 08/04-08 Vermont

OCT.

- ☐ 10/07: Chris and Skylar's wedding
- ☐ 10/14: Homecoming

NOV.

- ☐ 11/23: Thanksgiving

DEC.

- ☐ 12/06

"WHAT IF MY JOURNAL DOESN'T LAST FOR A FULL YEAR?"

When you start your dot journal, it's impossible to know how long a single notebook will last you. Many people's journals get them through an entire year. Meanwhile, I fill one every three months or so. My advice: Plan that your notebook is going to last for the rest of the current year, but know that it's not a big deal if it doesn't.

So, what does that look like? In my case, it means duplicating any spreads that are tied to the entire calendar year every time I start a new notebook during that year. For example, I want my book list to include every book I read in 2017. So when I set up my second notebook of the year, I re-created the page in the new notebook and copied all the books I'd finished in the first three months of the year from my first notebook. Then I added to that list as I completed more books. Same thing in my third notebook. (But I *don't* go back and add to the list in the first notebook.) I do the same thing for my other yearlong lists and spreads. While this might sound like a hassle, it actually only takes about twenty minutes to do when I'm setting up my new journal. I like this approach because it works whether you use one notebook for the year, or five.

I also don't worry about filling every single page in my notebook. So if it's, say, the end of June, and I have twenty pages left in my notebook, I'll start a new notebook on July 1—because I know that I can't fit an entire month in just twenty pages, and I'd rather not split a month across two notebooks. But it's really a matter of personal preference. If you'd rather fill every page, you can either rewrite your monthly pages for the month that's getting split up, or reference and update spreads in your old notebooks for a few weeks.

I did find myself faced with a dilemma when I needed to start a new notebook in December 2016. My first instinct was to use that same notebook for January and February of 2017 . . . but then I realized that transferring and updating those yearlong lists could get rather unwieldy. So I decided to go ahead and start a new journal *just* for the month of December. I knew doing it this way would mean leaving a lot of blank pages in my December 2016 notebook, but I figured it was worth it for better organization in the long run. Plus, knowing I had so many pages to fill actually encouraged me to write more, and I went from writing a half page of diary notes each day to writing three or four pages a day . . . so, win-win! That said, could I have made it work the other way? Absolutely.

Bottom line: Do whatever you want.

"

Mere facts and names and dates communicate
more than we suspect.
—HENRY DAVID THOREAU

"

CHAPTER 3

Monthly Spreads

A fter you've set up your future spread, you may want to create a few lists or other spreads that you plan to update over the course of the year. I'll talk about those more in chapter 9, but for now, let's focus on what will come after any and all yearly planning: the monthly spread.

This can be as simple as a *very* basic monthly calendar and a monthly task list. But you can make your monthly spread more or fewer pages, and can include all or just some of your events, tasks you need to tackle at some point in the month (like "make a doctor appointment" or "renew passport") or tasks assigned to specific dates ("send passport application by April 4"), monthly goals, and more.

For the record, I don't usually do monthly planning in my journal; I did when I first started, but I quickly realized that I didn't look at those pages much. Now I only do it for months when I have a lot going on. That's the beauty of this system—you can let any part of it go without guilt if you discover that it doesn't make sense for you.

When you're first setting up your dot journal, you'll *only* create a monthly spread for the current month. So if you're starting your dot journal in August, just do a monthly page for August. At the end of the month, you'll create the monthly spread for September, migrating unfinished tasks from August to the new September spread when you do.

Simple date list +
simple task list

One fast and unfussy way to create a monthly spread is to simply list all the dates down the left side of the page. Then you can write in the bigger events—travel, birthdays, appointments, etc.—next to the corresponding date.

The task list, which can either be on the same page or a separate page, contains all the big to-dos you want to check off in a given month. When creating your task list, you'll use the dot-journaling symbols . . . so the dot, the x, etc. (This is where the "migrate" and "scheduled" symbols really start to come in handy!)

September

F	1	
S	2	
S	3	
M	4	Labor Day
T	5	7 p.m. class
W	6	
T	7	
F	8	
S	9	
S	10	
M	11	
T	12	7 p.m. class
W	13	8 p.m. Club elections
T	14	6 p.m. baby-sit Riley
F	15	Jules bday, D.C. trip
S	16	D.C. trip
S	17	D.C. trip
M	18	
T	19	7 p.m. class
W	20	
T	21	
F	22	
S	23	
S	24	
M	25	
T	26	7 p.m. class
W	27	
T	28	
F	29	submit expense report
S	30	

TO DO^s

TO DOs
· return library books
· buy Jules bday gift
· book train to D.C.
· find a tailor

One page for tasks, goals, and events + a mini calendar

This is a good option if you decide you want to create a planner-style setup at the weekly or daily level (which I'll cover in more detail later). It also works well if you are someone who plans to maintain an electronic calendar for work meetings and events, a group I fall into. (Because my office relies heavily on Google calendars, and because our meetings frequently change, using a physical planner for every little work event doesn't make sense for me.) In either case, this spread makes tasks, reminders, goals, and motivation the focus of your monthly page.

july

S M T W T F S
1
2 3 4 5 6 7 8
9 10 11 12 13 14 15
16 17 18 19 20 21 22
23 24 25 26 27 28 29
30 31

tasks

- call cable company
- buy new sandals
- request August book club book from library
- follow up w/ advisory board
- research venues for surprise party
- renew license

events

6/30-7/9: Rhode Island vacation

7/13: doctor appt.

7/22: concert

7/25: eye doctor

goals

- take at least one 15-minute break each day
- be on time for work

work
hard &
be kind

Horizontal one-page calendar

Surprise—you can rotate your journal ninety degrees to maximize the space and create cool spreads! If you want to be able to see the entire month at a glance and don't need to keep track of very many events, a one-page calendar could work well for you. And if you want, you could use the opposite page for monthly tasks, goals, and general inspiration (written either vertically or horizontally).

M	T	W	T	F	S
				5 Pay Day	6	7 Knitting Club
1	2 office closed	3	4		
8 7 p.m. class	9	10	11 7 p.m. class	12	13 coffee w/ Ari	14
15	16 MLK Day	17	18 7 p.m. class	19 Pay Day	20	21
22 7 pm class	23	24	25 7 p.m. class	26	27	28
29 7 p.m. class	30	31			

dule call w/ Casey
nit receipts to
rance company
d an accountant
d library card
oose dates for work
ssions
t oil changed

"When I dare to be powerful, to use my strength in the service of my vision, then it becomes less and less important whether I am afraid."

– Audre Lorde

goals
· work out 3x/week
· read two books
· call mom every week

next month
· buy Alex bday gift
· book club feb. 18th

Two-page calendar layout

If you're using your dot journal as your main calendar/planner, you may want to devote two full pages to your monthly spread. That will give you plenty of room to write appointments, events, deadlines, and meetings. The example here adds a color-coding system, which makes it easier to spot certain items at a glance (and it looks nice!), but the spread works perfectly well in a single color.

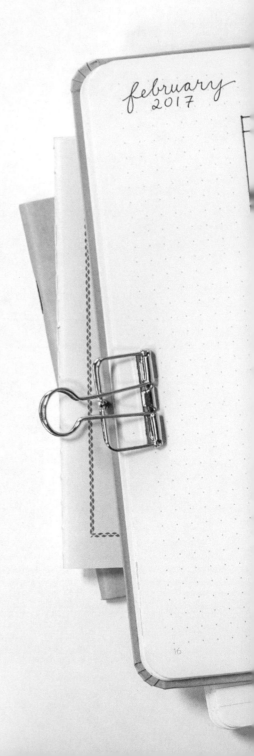

february
2017

16

Sun.	Mon.	Tues.	Weds.	Thurs.	Fri.	Sat.
			1	**2**	**3** 5:30 p.m. food bank shift Pay Day!	**4** 2 p. clu...
	6 7 p.m. class	**7**	**8** · register for conference 7 p.m. class	**9**	**10** 4 p.m. team happy hour 5:30 p.m. food bank shift	**11**
	13 7 p.m. class	**14**	**15** 2:30 p.m. design meeting 7 p.m. class	**16** 5:30 p.m. alumni happy hour	**17** 11 a.m. meeting w/ Noel Pay Day!	**18**
19 Jordan's bday	**20** Presidents' Day	**21**	**22** 7 p.m. class	**23**	**24** 5:30 p.m. food bank shift	
26	**27** 7 p.m. class	**28**				

"SHOULD I HAVE SEPARATE JOURNALS FOR DIFFERENT AREAS OF MY LIFE?"

Nah. But also . . . maybe?

After I started dot journaling, I noticed that some people kept more than one dot journal. They had their main dot journal, and then a different one for, say, their blog, or their small business. When I first saw this, I thought, *I finally got on board with the idea of putting my work and home tasks and diary in a single notebook, and now you're telling me I can have multiple notebooks? NOPE.* I didn't even consider it. First, I was worried that unless I carried both notebooks with me all the time, I'd get stuck in a situation where I didn't have the right one—which would defeat the entire purpose of this new system of organization. And as much as I would loooooove an excuse to buy multiple notebooks, I was less into the idea of needing to carry two notebooks with me at all times. However! I recognize that my feelings on this matter were heavily influenced by the fact that *I don't have a car.*

If you, like me, have a ninety-minute daily commute that involves a great deal of walking and public transportation, then the idea of carrying two notebooks is probably a nonstarter. (And that's fine, because it's definitely not necessary! I really can't overstate how much I like having everything in a single notebook.) If, on the other hand, you can travel from home to work to class to the grocery store with a tote full of notebooks and zero fear of developing permanent shoulder pain because that tote mostly sits on the front seat of your very spacious car . . . then having more than one notebook might make sense for you. I can tell you that if I were back in college, I'd probably have my main dot-grid hardcover journal, and would then use this dot journal *system* in a bunch of separate softcover notebooks that don't cost $15 a piece.

If you're leaning toward having multiple notebooks, you may be interested in another option: buying an empty journal cover that has a system of elastic bands inside it, bands that make it possible to slip multiple softcover notebooks in and out. This arrangement (often called a "traveler's notebook" online, after Traveler's Company, which popularized the style) is great if you want separate notebooks for different areas of interest, but want to keep all of them with you most of the time. You could, say, have a work notebook, a personal notebook, a sketchbook, and a notebook for your classes—one blank, one lined, one dotted, etc.—but you can corral them and tote them around in this single "notebook." It's basically just a smaller, more elegant Trapper Keeper.

Anyway, like pretty much everything with regard to dot journaling, whether you should use multiple notebooks comes down to personal preference, and what makes the most sense with your lifestyle.

CHAPTER 4

Monthly Habit Trackers

Habit tracking is one way to dot journal that has emerged and taken off as more people have started using the system, and it's one of my favorites. (Whenever I show people my dot journal, their faces light up the moment I flip to the habit tracker.) Because . . . *cool*, right?!

Along with giving you an excuse to create some very cool-looking layouts, habit trackers are an excellent way to visualize the progress you're making on your personal goals. You can track the things you want to be doing more of (cooking dinner at home, taking walks, reading) and things you want to be doing less of (eating fast food, swearing, drinking several cocktails and then shopping online, a thing that I have definitely never done because that would be crazy, ha ha ha).

I tend to set monthly goals for myself, so creating a habit tracker at the monthly level works well for me. And since I'm only making
one spread for each month, I can spend a little more time setting
it up. That said, you can absolutely do weekly trackers (or weekly
and monthly), and some people also do daily trackers for things like
water intake or medications. Totally your call!

Habit trackers are particularly helpful for health-related behaviors, as well as finances and chores, but I'll show layouts designed
specifically for those topics in later chapters. For now, here are
some ideas for more general habit trackers.

Horizontal monthly tracker for all habits

I love this style of tracker because it's such a creative way to use the space and the dot-grid pattern, and because you can track a ton of habits in it. It takes a few more minutes to set up than some of the other layouts, but it's *really* cool and fun to use.

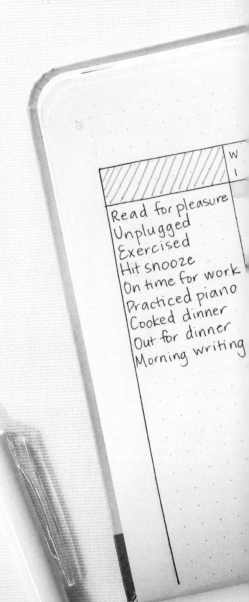

March Habits

S S M T W T F S S M T W T F S S M T W T F S S M T W T F S M T W T F
S S M T W T F S S M T W T F S S M T W T F S M T W T F
4 5 6 7 8 9 10 11 12 13 14 15 16 17 18 19 20 21 22 23 24 25 26 27 28 29 30 31

X pay r...
X pay student
☒ 2:30 p.m. desi
  work out
↗ buy dog food
↗ work on HO
request vac
sign up for

Vertical monthly tracker for all habits

If you want to be able to see all of your habits in one place but don't want to have to turn your notebook to the side to view them, you might prefer a vertical setup like this one. (This is the layout I currently use, though I just write the first letter of each habit instead of the full word because it looks cleaner that way.)

march
2017

	Read	Unplugged	Exercised	Hit snooze	Piano	Booze	Dinner out	Chores
1								
2								
3								
4								
5								
6								
7								
8								
9								
10								
11								
12								
13								
14								
15								
16								
17								
18								
19								
20								
21								
22								
23								
24								
25								
26								
27								
28								
29								
30								
31								

Single page with multiple trackers

Instead of putting all your habits in a single tracker, you could also give each habit its own tracker; this setup is a little easier to read, and is nice if you don't want to mix the things you're trying to do more of with the things you're trying to do less of in a single tracker. Once you've engaged in the habit, you can either cross that day out, or color the box in. (And if there are some days when you don't want or need to track the habit, you could just black those out in advance.) If you want to be able to glance at the page and know very quickly how well you're doing with regard to a specific behavior or goal, this is a really fantastic layout.

P.S. Because this spread (and the tracker on page 62) is written vertically on a single page, it can easily be set up opposite one of the single-page monthly layouts from chapter 3 to create a cohesive and beautiful two-page monthly log.

September

NO SPEND

1	2	3	4	5	6	7	8	9	10
11	12	13	14	15	16	17	18	19	20
21	22	23	24	25	26	27	28	29	30

WORK OUT

1	2	3	4	5	6	7	8	9	10
11	12	13	14	15	16	17	18	19	20
21	22	23	24	25	26	27	28	29	30

ON TIME FOR WORK

1	2	3	4	5	6	7	8	9	10
11	12	13	14	15	16	17	18	19	20
21	22	23	24	25	26	27	28	29	30

PRACTICED PIANO

1	2	3	4	5	6	7	8	9	10
11	12	13	14	15	16	17	18	19	20
21	22	23	24	25	26	27	28	29	30

READ BOOKS

1	2	3	4	5	6	7	8	9	10
11	12	13	14	15	16	17	18	19	20
21	22	23	24	25	26	27	28	29	30

ALL MEALS @ HOME

1	2	3	4	5	6	7	8	9	10
11	12	13	14	15	16	17	18	19	20
21	22	23	24	25	26	27	28	29	30

Mini monthly tracker

If you don't have very many habits to track, you could add a mini habit tracker to your monthly calendar page. I like this option because it keeps everything for the month in a single layout, meaning you don't have to flip pages as often.

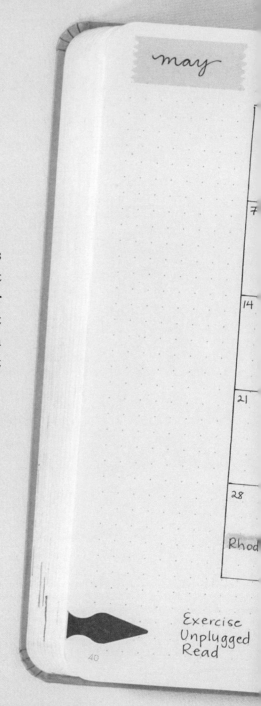

Sun	Mon	Tues	Weds	Thur	Fri	
	1	2	3	4	5	
8	9		10	11	12	13
15	16		17	18	19	20
22	23		24	25	26	27
				Rhode Island		
29	30		31			

and

2 3 4 5 6 7 8 9 10 11 12 13 14 15

16 17 18 19 20 21 22 23 24 25 26 27 28 29 30 31

JOURNALING BY THE NUMBERS

12: number of books in Marcus Aurelius' *Meditations*, which was written between 170 and 180 AD, and is credited as the first surviving diary

381–384 AD: years that Egeria, a Gallic pilgrim, wrote a travel journal as an ongoing letter to her friends back home

1450: year that Luca Landucci, an apothecary in Florence, Italy, wrote the first modern diary

176: number of unknown plants and wildflowers that explorers Lewis and Clark noted in their journals

15: number of notebooks that Charles Darwin had with him in 1831 when he began a nearly five-year trip around the world, notebooks he would later say "determined my whole career"

116,080: number of words Darwin wrote in said notebooks

15: age at which Beatrix Potter began writing in a diary, a habit she kept up from 1881 to 1897, in a code known only to her

1958: year that a man named Leslie Linder cracked the code and made it possible to read Potter's diaries

10: number of gifts that Anne Frank received for her thirteenth birthday on June 12, 1942, one of which was a diary

30 million: number of copies that Anne Frank's *The Diary of a Young Girl* has sold worldwide since its publication

91: number of years that Colonel Ernest Loftus kept a daily diary, which currently holds the Guinness World Record for the longest-kept diary

$30.8 million: final price for which a seventy-two-page notebook belonging to Leonardo da Vinci, called the *Codex Hammer*, sold at auction in 1994; the buyer was Bill Gates

1988: year that author Bruce Chatwin referred to his simple black notebook—which had rounded corners, a strap, and a pocket inside the back flap, and which was popular with artists in France—as a "moleskine" in his book *The Songlines*

15 million: total number of copies of the Bridget Jones books that have been sold worldwide

74: number of pounds Bridget Jones gains over the course of one year in *Bridget Jones's Diary*

72: number of pounds Bridget Jones loses over the course of that same year

CHAPTER 5

Weekly Spreads

ike habit trackers, weekly spreads have become popular as more people have taken up dot journaling. In fact, a lot of people do the bulk of their dot journaling at the weekly level; they may not have daily pages at all, or they'll use their daily pages strictly for diary entries. (For others—myself included—the weeklies are a high-level overview, and the dailies are where the nitty-gritty happens.) Working mostly from your weeklies can be a great option if you don't want to create a new spread each morning; just set it up at the beginning of the week, and then you're good to go!

The weekly spreads are where the dot journal system *really* starts to shine. I'm always amazed by how much information you can pack into one or two pages if you use the space creatively.

Multiunit two-page spread

This is a popular layout, in part because it can hold a *ton* of info. If you find you want more space to write each day's tasks and events, you could remove the boxes at the bottom of the left-side page, or just make them smaller.

may 15 - may

Mon.	Tues.
5/15	5/16

☐ all-hands @ 9:30
☐ check-in w/
Kyle @ 3:45
✗ reschedule PT
✗ read article
✗ submit report
for review
✗ sign up for Fri.
cycling class
✗ book hotel for
Taylor + Tyler's
wedding
/ hike w/ Alex

☐ artic
· prin
exa
· foll
des
· ora
∧ fin
✗ fol
✗ go
cor
re
☐ S
@

Notes

— Alex bailed on our
Monday at the last
and it turned into t
thing. I'm just so s
flakiness! We made
though.
— Noel has been driv
at work this week..
cold.
— Coffee with Chris
perfect mid-week
just what I neede

44

Weds.
5/17

e 12 — × morning run
ctice. — ☐ 10 a.m. design
     team meeting
with — · buy Sam new
eam   bear
e receipts — × ask IT about
's bear   missing files
dry — · finalize purchase
gh Noel's   order
ts on — × work session
    ☐ coffee w/ Chris
etti Dinner

Thurs.
5/18

× follow up with IT
· update report title page
· email Casey
< schedule call w/ HQ
☐ production mtg. @ 10:30 a.m.
> bring coupon for Tracy

Fri.
5/19

☐ 7 a.m. cycling class
× bring coupon for Tracy
· sign up for training session
☐ 4 p.m. team happy hour
· send application to HQ
× picnic planning meeting poster

Sat./Sun.
5/20

· laundry
× hike w/ Sam
☐ Date Night

5/21

· grocery store
· change sheets
☐ BBQ
· take trash out

Gratitude

M: snuggles with Sam, my bed
T: my family
W: veggies from the farmers market
T: my job
F: the kind person who found/returned my wallet
S: grandma's home-made banana pudding recipe
S: good friends and good brisket

on
te
HUGE
of the
ater

e nuts
ot and

the
ne-up...

	M	T	W	T	F	S	S
Exercise	M	T	☒	T	☒	☒	S
Unplug	M	T	☒	☒	F	S	S
Read	☒	T	W	T	F	S	S
10,000 steps	☒	T	☒	☒	☒	☒	S
Eat @ home	☒	T	☒	☒	F	S	S

Weekly events, divided by type

I love this spread, which is great for people who don't have much to write each day, and/or want to be able to visually distinguish between personal and work events. As an alternative, you could designate one column as events and one as tasks, one as school and one as work, etc.

home		work
☐ dry cleaning ready	MON. 15 MAY	☒ 11 a.m. coffee ☒ 3:45 check in mtg.
	TUE 16 MAY	
☒ 6 p.m. running club	WED. 17 MAY	
	THUR 18 MAY	☒ 9 a.m. all-hands mtg. ☒ happy hour
☒ 6 p.m. running club	FRI. 19 MAY	☐ wireframe due ☐ happy hour
	SAT. 20 MAY	
☐ brunch w/ Ari	SUN. 21 MAY	

Multiple-column weekly layout

If you looked at the previous spread and thought, *OK, that, but divided into work, school,* and *home, plus with some space for additional lists*, then this might be a good layout for you!

05/15 - 05/21

WORK

15	9:30 a.m: all-han
16	
17	work 1-5
18	work 4-9
19	
20	work 8-5
21	work 4-9

SCHOOL

11 a.m.: Econ
8 a.m.: Bio Lab 9 a.m.: Bio 11 a.m.: Women's Studies
11 a.m.: Econ 8 p.m.: study group
9 a.m.: Bio 11 a.m.: Women's Studies
· internship application

HOME

· mail bills
· work out
8 a.m.: physical therapy
· work out
> grocery store 7 p.m.: baby-sit Riley
· grocery store · get car washed
· work out

DO
- · read Ch.14-19 for Econ.
- x read Coontz essay for WS
- x review contract
- x print + sign contract
- · research sewing classes
- ^ find original birth certificate
- · get passport photos taken
- · sign up for training session
- · bring book for Kyle
- ^ find new doctor
- · make posters for food drive
- x cash check
- · call Mom + Dad
- · buy gift card for Stacy
- < get a haircut

BUY
- · stamps
- · body wash
- · yarn

NOTES
- — Econ is so hard and I hate it
- — Made it to the gym BE my 8 a.m. lab on Tuesday
- — It was SO cold this we
- — Ran into Cory on Friday on my way home + we ma tentative plans to have c next week

Single-page multiunit spread

This setup gives you space to write events and appointments for the week, and leaves room for items that aren't tied to a specific day/time. You could also replace the notes section with a mini tracker or a mantra, or use it to note any upcoming tasks you want to remember to add to the following week's spread.

10/08-10/14

S 8	2:00: volunteer shift
M 9	9:30: all-hands meeting 3:45: check-in w/ Kyle
T 10	12:00: Article Club 5:30: Spaghetti Dinner 7:00: class
W 11	11:00: group planning meeting
T 12	10:30: production meeting 11:30: marketing meeting
F 13	7:00: drive home
S 14	Homecoming

tasks

- do laundry
- send Leslie thank you card
- grocery store
- confirm pet sitter
- reschedule lawn treatment
- buy face wash
- get cash
- car snacks
- print & sign docs
- order photos

notes

- Felt so anxious about everything. I had to get done before my trip
- Ari decided not to go home for Homecoming so I had to make the drive alone & then I got a flat tire...luckily it was in the driveway
- We lost 31-0... it was a total bloodbath

86

neu

- garr
loquac
- vert
change
- capa
great
- bonh
ciation
- malf
by a p
- mal
misuse
the us
intend
- spos
- amel
- uxor
- effu
- nug
- laco
words,
ous (p
- hoa
- may
- prot
- adju
- abj
- incu
mind
- mo
- rec
- abr

Grid + mini calendar

This is how I set up my weekly page; I love being able to see a list of big tasks I want to accomplish at work during the week, and I've found that it's easiest for me to stay on top of all my weekly tasks when they are separated by category. Some weeks, I'll change what I put in the bottom two boxes, or I'll limit the spread to just two columns. Creating my weekly spread is the last thing I do every Sunday night before bed, and it helps me transition from weekend mode back to work mode.

june

S	M	T	W	T	F	S
				1	2	3
4	5	6	7	8	9	10
11	12	13	14	15	16	17
18	19	20	21	22	23	24
25	26	27	28	29	30	

work

- · study for certification exam
- < schedule Kyle's review
- · finalize presentation
- × follow up w/ HR

home

- · water plants
- × mail passport application
- ∧ fix picture frame
- · send Taylor + Tyler's wedding gift

events

- ☐ Shakespeare in the park
- ☐ food bank shift
- ☐ physical therapy
- ☐ movie date
- ☐ Reading Day @ Riley's school

buy

- × wedding card
- × wood glue
- · allergy meds
- · trash bags
- · salt
- · matches

"WHAT IF I MAKE A MISTAKE?"

Spoiler alert: You will definitely make mistakes in your dot journal! Some will be minor, but big mistakes—like, say, spelling "February" wrong in a page header, or starting the month on the wrong day when you're making a calendar—will happen, too. Messing up is always a bummer, but I've picked up a few tips along the way for making it less disastrous:

1. **Use correction tape.** It's classic for a reason! Correction tape is especially good for smaller mistakes, like spelling errors and smeared pen.

2. **Put a sticker or a piece of washi tape over the mistake.** Pretend it never happened.

3. **Cover the entire page with a fresh piece of paper.** Get some clean paper or cardstock, trim it to fit the page, and glue it or tape it down. Then you can either rewrite whatever you had planned on the fresh paper, or you can put something else on it (like an inspirational quote or a drawing) and restart your planned spread on the next page.

4. **Tape or glue the pages together.** The page with the mistake is dead to you now. Let us never speak of it again.

5. **Write important text (like headers) and/or more detailed layouts lightly in pencil first.** You certainly don't have to do this, but it's a good idea if you're a perfectionist or if you have a habit of making cringe-worthy mistakes. Once you're happy with how everything looks, write over it with pen and then erase the pencil marks. (Heads up: If you go this route, be sure to give the ink plenty of time to dry before you erase the pencil. My impatience has led to so many smeared layouts. Do not be like me.)

6. **Be careful about tearing pages out.** I've found that tearing out a single page in some notebooks can lead to wrinkled and loose pages throughout the rest of the book. Not worth it.

7. **Let it go.** Seriously, give yourself permission to move on. I always feel annoyed when I make a mistake, but within a couple pages, I've forgotten about it entirely.

"

In the journal I do not just express myself more openly
than I could to any person; I create myself. The journal
is a vehicle for my sense of selfhood. It represents me
as emotionally and spiritually independent. Therefore
(alas) it does not simply record my actual, daily life but
rather—in many cases—offers an alternative to it.

—SUSAN SONTAG

"

CHAPTER 6

Daily Spreads

Now it's time for the fun stuff: making your daily to-do list! You'll probably spend a decent amount of time looking at your daily spread, so it's worth it to find a layout that really works for you, and that you actually like looking at. If you don't have much time to spend creating your spread each day, you'll probably be happiest with something simple and straightforward. If you know you'd enjoy the process of creating something that requires more time and effort (and maybe a ruler or some markers), you can do something more complex. And, of course, you can experiment with different styles of dailies at any point in the journal, since you get to make a new one each day. Here is a range of ideas to get you started.

My daily setup

I write the date at the top of the page with a colored pen (usually gray, but I've been known to go wild and use olive green or navy blue), and then write all my work-related tasks and events on the left side of the page in black pen. Just to the right of the center of the page, I write my nonwork tasks and events for the day, also in black pen. (Occasionally, I do my daily tasks as a single column and write work items in black pen and nonwork items in gray pen—again, I'm pretty wild!) The page functions as my to-do list throughout the day and helps me stay organized and focused.

Then, at night, I skip a couple of lines after my last task, write "Notes" in the same color pen as I wrote the date, and log more diary-like notes below that, using the "—" symbol. Once I finish writing my notes for the night, I go to the next blank page, write the next day's date at the top, migrate the tasks I didn't get to, and start the whole routine again.

february 13, 2017

- ☒ all-hands meeting
- ☓ reach out to Harper
- ☓ finish presentation notes
- ☑ check-in w/ Kyle
- › email volunteers
- ☒ planning call w/ Noel
- ‹ happy hour reservation
- · respond to Ali
- ☓ check Alpha Board posts

- › post office
- ☓ work out
- ☒ class
- › light bulbs

notes

— Managed to get to the gym before work this AM, which was a victory! Did 30 minutes on the elliptical trainer; I pushed it pretty hard but felt really great afterward.

— Am feeling really frustrated w/ Kyle; our check-in didn't happen today (Kyle was sick and worked from home) so I couldn't even try the new communication tactics Noel suggested.

— Alpha Board was a COMPLETE mess today, which meant my afternoon was no fun

— Class tonight was pretty fun... I'm finally getting more comfortable and making friends

— Sam seemed annoyed with me today, probably for being gone so much this weekend

— Taylor called me when I was on my way home and we had a nice catch-up session

d in

t
n
d
us
led to

be

was
like
+ too

iskey,
rench
Ice

itched
for

tched
the

Daily spread, take two

Instead of writing your tasks as a single column, this spread has you writing them in a horizontal, paragraph-like format instead—a cool twist on the standard vertical format that you see in most dot journals (and most to-do lists in general). Doing it this way takes up less space, leaving you plenty of room to start the next day directly under the previous day if you want to. It also means that a single notebook will probably last you considerably longer than it would otherwise.

I prefer to create my daily setup at night, because then I can add things I need to remember to do before I leave the house in the morning, and I can get started working on my tasks as soon as I get to the office. Plus, I find that writing down tasks before I go to bed means they are less likely to keep me up at night. But a lot of people enjoy journaling in the morning, and prefer to set up their daily pages then. Figure out what works best for you and go with it!

January 03, 2017

x email Ali | · follow up w/Harper | · schedule
budget meeting | · register for certification
exam | · update bank info w/gym | ☒ team
happy hour @ 4:30 | ☑ food bank shift @ 5:30

notes

— Had a pretty slow day at work today. Caught
up on emails and am almost at inbox zero! It
only took me two months. | — Was able to text w/
Alex a little bit while I was at work, which
is always a treat. Excited about our date
tomorrow night. | — Didn't make it to the gym
all week, but hoping to make up for that this
weekend. | — Team happy hour was fun! I haven't
been able to attend one in a while, but finally
did and got some much-needed venting time with
Leslie and Casey.

January 04, 2017

☐ Knitting Club @ 2 p.m. | · grocery store | · pick
up prescription

Hourly agenda

This layout has an hourly breakdown so you can write out your full schedule, the way you would in a traditional planner. The right side of the page remains free for whatever you'd like to put there; I added tasks and a little diary entry to this one, but you could just as easily use that space to track daily habits (like exercise, water intake, medication), mood, etc.

03.31.17

6

7 gym
  shower
8

9 class

10 |

11 ↓

12 meet Ari for lunch

1 review session

2
  haircut
3

4 volunteer shift

5 ↓

6 dinner w/ Alex

7 baby-sit Riley

8 |

9 | PBS special

10 ↓

11

---

tasks

- · get cash
- x read Ch. 8-13
- · pick up Rx.
- · toilet paper
- x water plants
- / call insurance company

---

notes

- Workout wasn't great (I was running late/felt rushed) but whatever... I did it!
- Alex and I are both so busy this week, so we did a quick dinner before I went to the Henderson's
- Feeling a little bummed about my haircut...it's much shorter than I wanted. Alex said it looks okay, but Riley said (as a compliment!) that I look like a mushroom ☺

Multiple days per page

Is this spread a "daily" or a "weekly"? You tell me! I tend to think of it as a weekly, but many others call it a daily, so I'm including it here. Regardless of what you call it, you can either create the entire layout on Sunday night and fill it in as the week goes on (which is what I've shown here), or you can start each new day directly under the previous day's list, making the most of the space.

mon. 3/20
x pay student loan
x 9:30 all-hands meeting
x 3:45 check-in with Kyle
x send paperwork to Noel fo
> finalize box order
. submit T-shirt design req
. call Jordan back
— Had wild dream last night
by a shark
— Worked out (30 min run, 30 m

tues. 3/21
x 4 p.m. Women in Science lectu
x 5:30 p.m. Spaghetti Dinner
x finalize box order
^ check posts on Alpha Board
x submit updated budget
x RSVP for engagement party
— Ari came to Spaghetti Dinner w,
had a study session

weds. 3/22
x call airline for Noel
x pay electric bill
x check Alpha Board
^ Alpha Board replies
. follow up on IT ticket
— Worked out this morning at 7:30...u
boot camp class than usual and it was

thurs 3/23

- [x] 10 a.m. production meeting
- [x] 11:30 a.m. marketing meeting
- prepare audio for packaging
- > get price adjustment
- — Talked with Alex for a while tonight and it was great... I was finally able to open up about everything going on with my parents & I feel a lot better now.

fri. 3/24

- x drop off dry cleaning
- [✓] 4 p.m. team happy hour
- x get price adjustment
- send design feedback
- — Attended review session this afternoon. I thought it was going to be a waste of time but it was actually pretty helpful!

sat. 3/25

- x pick up dry cleaning
- x vacuum
- > clean kitchen
- > clean bathroom
- x grocery store
- [x] hike w/ Alex

sun. 3/26

- [x] brunch w/ Taylor & Tyler
- [x] 7 p.m. yoga class
- clean kitchen
- clean bathroom

oval

Alex got attacked

yoga)

and then we

o a different
ard.

THE FATHER OF THE MODERN DIARY

Samuel Pepys (pronounced "peeps") is one of history's most prolific diarists. After writing his first diary entry on January 1, 1660, he filled 3,102 pages over the next nine years, missing only *fourteen days* in that time. He wrote during a turbulent time in London that included the plague of 1665 and the Great Fire of 1666, and he documented politics, current events, and scenes from his personal life in vibrant, unselfconscious prose.

His diaries contain some real gems, and by "gems" I mean things that made me mutter, "Wow, what an asshole." On January 9, 1663, Pepys *tore apart and burned* his wife's diary because he didn't like that she "wrote in English, and most of it true, of the retirednesse of her life and how unpleasant it is." Yes, this dude who is famous for writing diaries destroyed his wife's diary because *he didn't like the true things she wrote about him in it.* Also! On June 3, 1666, the still-married Mr. Pepys wrote in his diary of what he did with one Mrs. Martin: "Did what je Bourdais avec her, both devante and backward, which is also muy bon plazer"—one of the *numerous* affairs he recorded in his diary. I'm not sure what is worse: that he cheated on his wife, or that he documented it in cheesy faux French. *Le woof.*

CHAPTER 7

Using Your Dot Journal as a Diary

To some degree, your entire dot journal is a diary. While writing things down quickly using short phrases and symbols may seem at odds with what you've always understood a diary to be—"What do you *mean* I should just sum up my wedding in three words?!"—the historical record shows otherwise. The way people keep diaries has changed over time. Though we now tend to think of diaries as a private space for writing paragraph after paragraph of our innermost thoughts, that's a relatively modern development. Historian Margo Culley writes that, prior to the late nineteenth century in the United States, diaries were semipublic documents where people (usually women) wrote the history of their families and communities—"they recorded in exquisite detail the births, deaths, illnesses, visits, travel, marriages, work, and unusual occurrences that made up the fabric of their lives," she says. And in terms of formatting, well . . . many of the diaries from the sixteenth and seventeenth century looked *remarkably* like dot journals.

THE DIARY OF MARY VIAL HOLYOKE

Apr. 7 [1770]. Mr. Fisk Buried.

23. Went with Mr. Eppes to Mrs. Thomas. Took Down Beds.

26. Put Sals Coat in ye frame.

27. Made mead. At the assembly.

May 14. Mrs. Mascarene here & Mrs. Crowninshield. Taken very ill. The Doctor bled me. Took an anodyne.

15. Kept my Bed all day.

17. Brought to Bed at 12 of a son.

19. The Baby taken with fits the same as ye others. Nurse came. Mrs. Vans Died.

20. The Baby very ill. I first got up.

21. It Died at 11 °clock A.M. Was opened. The Disorder was found to Be in the Bowels. Aunt Holyoke died.

22. Training. Mother Pickman here. Mrs. Sarjant yesterday.

23. My dear Baby buried.

28. Mrs. Pickman, Miss Dowse Drank tea here. Mrs. Jones, Lowell, Brown, Cotnam, Miss Cotnam & Miss Gardnre Called to see me.

29. Wrote to Boston and Cambridge. Mrs. Savage Brought to Bed. The widow Ward lost 2 children with ye Throat Distemper from May 25th to May 29th.

30. Cato went to Boston and returned.

Like other diaries from that time period, there is very little "I" and basically zero emotion in Mary Vial Holyoke's writing, even as she's writing about the death of her babies (she would lose eight of her twelve children during her lifetime). But in the twentieth century, that changed, and diaries became more "me"-centric—aka the style that I imitated for most of my life. While this format has its appeal, you could also argue that things went too far in the opposite direction. In any case, the dot journal falls firmly in the center of these two styles, which is what I love about it.

Here are some ways to bring the modern, more narrative style of diary writing to your dot journal.

My diary setup

As I mentioned in the last chapter, I log my diary entries just below my tasks in a notes section every night. I typically use the "—" note symbol when I'm doing this, but I'll use the event symbol when I'm writing about something that feels particularly significant. Sometimes, each line is short and quick (like "slept well last night" or "UGGGHHHHHHHH"); other times, the note symbol is followed by several full sentences. Some nights, I'll just write a few lines in this section; other nights, I'll fill four pages. It really just depends.

From time to time, something major will happen and I won't have time to write about it before bed. In those instances, I leave the notes section blank and skip a page (or more, if I know I'm going to have a lot to say) before starting the next day's daily log. Then I go back and fill in the notes the next day. (I usually mark "Notes" with an asterisk on those days to signify that they were written later.)

february 12, 2017

x run a load of laundry
x work out
[x] Jules + Quinn leave
x order new glasses
[x] hang out w/ Alex

notes

- OMG, today was the coldest weather we've had in a LONG time.
- Got up before everyone else to do a quick workout
- Today was Jules + Quinn's last day in town; Quinn made us eggs, bacon, biscuits, homemade whipped cream, and berries and everything was SO delicious
- Dropped them off at the train station, then headed to Alex's place
- Went and picked out new glasses; they should be here in a week
- Alex took me to Clyde's for lunch. I thought it was the same place where we'd once met up for drinks like eight years ago, but it turns out it wasn't. (I wasn't too far off, though...that place is around the corner.)
- I had three Fire on Ice cocktails (cinnamon whiskey, amaretto, ginger beer, and Crème de Noyaux) and a French dip sandwich. It was all so good and the Fire on Ice cocktails were perfect for this weather
- Went back to Alex's, changed into cozies, and watched "Inception," which I'd been in the mood to watch for a while
- Pretty sure I almost broke Alex's back
- Later we ordered Chinese food for dinner and watched a bunch of nature documentaries about penguins / the Southern Hemisphere
- It was a really, really great day

18

[x] all-
x rea
x fin
[/] ch
> em
[x] pla
< ha
· res
x che

not

- Ma
which
traine
great
- Am
didn't
home)
tactics
- Alp
mean
- Clas
more
- Sam
being
- Tay
and w

Daily writing prompts

If you love the *idea* of keeping a diary but never know exactly what to write when faced with a blank page, then setting up a page with a list of writing prompts could be helpful. Here are some to get you started.

A lot of people find it easy to maintain a diary when they are having a rough time (sooo many angsty post-breakup entries!), but aren't as inspired to write when everything is going well. I have definitely fallen into this trap throughout my life. But what I like about dot journaling is that I'm motivated to write every day, regardless of my mood. Not writing about the good stuff—even when that good stuff is routine, or when you think you don't really have much to say—means you could be missing out on writing about big, important parts of your life that you'll wish you had included later.

journaling prompts

- Something unexpected that happened today was...

- I don't like that I'm feeling X about Y...

- An amazing thought I had today was...

- Something I wish I'd done differently was...

- One thought I couldn't get rid of today was...

- A person I'm thinking about today is...

- Today I was grateful for...

Monthly diary setup

If you are struggling to write on a daily basis, a monthly diary entry (or a weekly one) might be more feasible. It's a manageable, low-key way to reflect on how you're feeling and to mentally prepare for whatever's next. You could flip back through previous dailies to help you remember everything you did throughout the month, and/or take inspiration from the following prompts.

- What did I learn this month?
- What did I accomplish this month?
- What surprised me this month?
- What day do I remember best from this month?
- Who played a big role in my life this month?
- What was my best moment? What was my worst?
- What do I wish I'd done differently?
- What did I start doing? What did I stop doing?
- What goals do I want to achieve next month?

№ 05.17

This month, I started working on Project Beta Fish, something I have wanted to do for SO long, but it's turning out to be so much more challenging than I expected. I thought the application was difficult, but HO BOY — that was just the beginning. I wish I'd known how much mental energy this would take up. Had I realized, I probably wouldn't have chosen this month to take on extra shifts at the food bank, or to help plan Taylor + Tyler's joint wedding shower. Woof. I'm exhausted.

There were a couple low moments this month. The first was when I came home and found Sam and Dakota in bed together. In my own bed! IN MY OWN HOUSE!!! The Project Beta Fish kick-off meeting was also rough. I got so stressed out and lost my temper in front of the children. I apologized to everyone, but I'm just so embarrassed. The best moment from this month was Taylor and Tyler's wedding shower. Even though the planning process was annoying at times, it was worth it in the end. They make such a great couple, and getting to meet Tyler's extended family at the shower was wonderful. I'm very excited for the wedding next month — I love these two so, so much and can't wait to see them tie the knot!

Next month, I expect Project Beta Fish to take up even more time, which means I'll have less time for Alex and Sam, which is a bummer, but I hope they'll be supportive since they know how much this means to me. I also want to get back to flossing every day! Such a small thing, but it really matters.

Separate diary section

If you don't want to mix daily task lists and diary entries—a perfectly reasonable desire if, say, you want to keep your dot journal open on your desk all day while you're at work—this is a simple alternative. Just start a diary section about half-way through your book. Then, whenever you write a new diary entry in that section, make a note of its page number somewhere on the corresponding day's task list—kind of like an endnote in a book. (This is also a useful habit for people who do most of their dot journaling at the weekly level, or who decide to keep separate notebooks.)

thurs.
06.13.17

- ☒ feed Casey's cats
- ☒ 10 a.m. production meeting
- ☒ 11:30 a.m. marketing meeting
- ☒ 5:30 p.m. alumni happy hour
- < schedule budget meeting
- ☒ check Alpha Board
- / go to bank
- > buy trash bags
- > reserve book club book
- ▷ 141

☒ Had physical therapy this morning. I feel like I'm finally making progress!
- The planning meeting today was really quite dramatic. Leslie finally took a firm stance on the Project Beta Fish problems and Harper got upset and was like "I feel so attacked right now" and Leslie didn't even bat an eye
- The new systems we've put in place for Alpha Board are helping a LOT... I feel a lot better about how we're handling issues
- My new shoes finally arrived! Glad that whole debacle is finally over.
- Had a dream last night I was the lifeguard at a lake filled with dolphins and ponies

---

- Started my day at Casey's place feeding the cats. I don't mind doing it, especially because Casey's condo has such an incredible view.
- I love getting there early enough that I can feed the cats and then sit on the patio with my cold brew coffee and read or write
- The weather this morning was great and I felt totally calm + peaceful sitting out there
- Wore my new shoes to work today and looked so good (if I do say so myself).
- Alpha Board is getting a ton of activity, so my day was super full.
- We had a strange incident this morning between two junior members and I had to figure out what to do but I think I ultimately made the right call
- The news today was absolutely bananas! Ended up having an annoying argument about it during happy hour.
- Sam is still having wild mood swings and I don't know what to do! Hoping everything is OK while we're away for Taylor + Tyler's wedding this weekend

"HOW HONEST SHOULD I BE IN MY DOT JOURNAL?"

I vote for being pretty honest.

I mean, listen: If writing down the truth about a certain situation could lead to actual harm coming your way if the wrong person were to read it, then *absolutely* play it safe. But if you're mostly just embarrassed by your own feelings, or worried that Future You is going to judge what Current You is writing, I'd encourage you to be candid, and to include a *lot* of details. (This also applies to your tasks and goals, too; be honest about what you want to do, what's motivating you, and what you do or don't want to accomplish.)

I recently reread my high school and college diaries, and I was struck by how little context I added to important moments. I assumed I would remember exactly who people were, and couldn't imagine forgetting the context in which day-to-day events were taking place. Yeah . . . I don't remember *at all*. There were also several instances where I was deliberately vague because I was uncomfortable writing down the truth for one reason or another, and now I have no idea what I was talking about. Sure, some of the more honest entries in my old diaries are *deeply* embarrassing—I'm turning red just thinking about them!—but, well . . . I've done some embarrassing things in my life! Looking back, cringing, and reassuring myself that I've grown and changed is kind of the point.

So what I'm saying is . . . yes, you should write all the sex stuff.

On the *other* hand . . . I would encourage you to not get too caught up in *authenticity*. For years, I had a lot of arbitrary rules in my head about diaries. I had to write about events on the exact day they happened, or I couldn't write about them at all. I couldn't add additional details to entries later, or make changes if I'd recorded something incorrectly. If I quoted someone, I had to remember their *exact* words (which meant I basically never quoted people). But these kinds of limitations can feel so stifling that you give up writing in your diary entirely. In hindsight, I wish I'd realized that there were no journal police looking over my shoulder and that these "rules" were entirely in my own head. Turns out, no one else really cares about them, or follows them.

I was recently surprised to learn that some of the world's most famous diaries were *heavily* updated by their authors at later points in time. Two years after she began her now-famous diary, Anne Frank began editing the earlier entries she'd written—after hearing on a radio broadcast that an exiled member of the Dutch government wanted to publish firsthand accounts of the war. She continued to write new entries but also ended up editing nearly two-thirds of her diary before she was arrested in August 1944. Her changes and additions provided context for future audiences and made her diary read more like a narrative. All that to say: *No* diary is "perfect" in its original form, *especially* not ones that weren't written by a professional writer with an audience in mind. And just like a "natural" makeup look usually involves a decent amount of makeup, most published diaries have been edited.

I'm not saying you should go back to a day you were really upset, cross everything out, and write, "Wow, who got ahold of my diary and wrote this crazy entry? Certainly not me, the person who is perfectly fine and definitely felt no emotions about this thing at all!" I'm just saying there's no shame in writing an entry for June 12 on, say, June 15.

ANNE FRANK DIARY ENTRY, ORIGINAL

This morning we were glad that the plumber didn't come, because his son who was in Germany and had returned, was having to go back again because he had received another call-up. Mr. Levinsohn came instead, he had to boil up test samples for Mr. Kugler. It wasn't very pleasant, because that person, just like the plumber, knows the whole house, so we had to be quiet as mice.

ANNE FRANK DIARY ENTRY, REVISED

The days are becoming very quiet here. Levinsohn, a small Jewish chemist and dispenser, works for Mr. Kugler in the kitchen. He knows the whole house very well and therefore we are always afraid that he'll take it into his head to have a peep in the old laboratory. We are as quiet as baby mice. Who, three months ago, would have guessed that quicksilver Anne would have to sit still for hours—and, what's more, could?

"I'M WORRIED SOMEONE ELSE IS GOING TO LOOK AT MY DOT JOURNAL AND DISCOVER A BUNCH OF NOT-FOR-THEIR-EYES INFORMATION."

I was lucky to grow up in a household where I didn't have to be too concerned about anyone reading my diary. My mom was awesome about giving me privacy, and when she said she would never read my diary, I knew I could believe her. I mistakenly assumed everyone shared her point of view, and I got a rude awakening in fifth grade when a cousin read my diary and then tore out a page that said (true!) things about her. I was shocked and furious. To read someone else's diary just struck me as a *massive* violation.

After that, I made it a point to tell anyone who might need to know that my diary is private, and that reading it would be a pretty unforgivable offense, which basically means: *If you read my diary and see something about yourself that you don't like, you don't get to be angry with me about it.* And I haven't had any other issues (that I know of!) with snoops.

Of course, not everyone is surrounded by people who respect their boundaries, and concerns about privacy are real and reasonable when starting your dot journal. Here are some tips for keeping people out:

1. **If your journal is private, tell that to roommates/partners/kids.** Some people might see an unfamiliar book and think, *Oh, huh, what's this?*, open it, and accidentally discover things they shouldn't have before they even realize what's happening. So let people know: "This is my dot journal! If you ever touch it, I will cut off your fingers." Then give them your best "I'm definitely not a serial killer . . . or *am* I?" smile, and go back to working on your newest spread like nothing happened.

2. **If you'd feel more comfortable locking up your journal when you don't have it with you . . . go ahead!** It's your heart on those pages, and you're allowed to feel protective.

3. **Be discreet.** If you leave your notebook on the kitchen table, open to a page where you've gone on a nasty rant about someone you live with . . . and then that person sees it and keeps reading, well . . . I'm Team No One in that instance.

4. **Write in code.** OK, I'm not saying you should learn Elvish for the sake of your dot journal . . . *but* if you already know runes, pigpen cipher, or even just shorthand (or have been wanting to learn any of these systems), then go for it! You could also write in

a different language if you know one. Sure, none of these methods are going to fool the CIA, but they will probably mean that any nosy people peeking over your shoulder will be sorely disappointed.

5. Don't turn your dot journal into forbidden fruit. I think part of the reason the people closest to me are disinterested in my dot journal is because (A) I'm pretty honest in real life, so people don't have a strong desire to dig deeper, and (B) I don't make a big deal out of it or treat it like some big cache of all my secrets. Basically, just be cool, guys.

"BUT WHAT IF I WANT TO SHARE THINGS I WROTE IN MY DOT JOURNAL WITH OTHER PEOPLE?"

Well, you wouldn't be the first person to feel that way! For hundreds of years, diaries were, to some degree, public—at least within a family. Victorian parents often read their daughters' diaries, and sometimes wrote notes to their daughters in them as well. Louisa May Alcott and her sisters read their diaries out loud. And girls in boarding school sometimes gathered together to write, shared what they wrote in their diaries about each other as a way to bond, and even wrote in each other's diaries.

While I personally wouldn't ever hand my whole notebook to someone else to peruse, I have no problem reading things aloud to other people on occasion, or texting photos of old passages to my friends from time to time. A friend of mine found that when she was having a serious disagreement with her husband, it was helpful for both of them if she wrote out her thoughts in the form of a letter in her diary, and then read it aloud to him. So if something like that feels right to you, then go for it!

You could also go all in with the *completely* open approach. Leo Tolstoy and his wife, Sonya, famously shared their diaries with each other for forty-two years of marriage. Did this affect what and how they wrote in their diaries? Undoubtedly. Did Leo once read a short story that Sonya wrote in her diary about three sisters in love with the same man, and then base the Rostov family in his novel *War and Peace* off of them? He most certainly did! But if they were both cool with this approach to diary keeping, then who am I to judge?

CHAPTER 8

Health and Fitness Spreads

The dot journal system is a natural fit for tracking health-related tasks and activities. While some of these are obvious (like using it to log workouts or meals), I'm a huge fan of using my dot journal to record basic things that I might otherwise overlook. As I've gotten older, I've begun paying more attention to everything from sleep and medications to caffeine, hygiene, and alcohol intake. Tracking problems (headaches, fatigue, anxiety, irritability) as they occur helps me spot patterns that could be signs of something bigger, *and* it comes in handy when my doctor inevitably asks me, "When did you first notice this?" Now I have receipts!

The trackers in this chapter—which were developed with input from clinical psychologist Andrea Bonior, PhD, and amazing health reporter (and friend of mine) Anna Borges—can motivate you, make it easier to stick to your goals, and, ultimately, help you take better care of your physical and mental health. "When your life and emotions feel so out of control or chaotic, there is something immensely therapeutic about organizing it into a systematic structure," Bonior says. "You lay things out in an aesthetically pleasing way and already it feels more manageable. Like you can really tackle it and make it through. It feels luxurious, too. It's like saying, 'I'm worth it. I'm worth this notebook and the time it takes to turn it into something beautiful.'"

Before you start tracking your health habits, set realistic goals so you don't get discouraged if you have an off day (or . . . *several* off days). Bonior says it's best not to go into this expecting that your tracker will look perfect at the end of the month. It's more important that it reflects your real life, and helps you improve.

Mega monthly tracker for everything

This setup takes the monthly tracking layout from chapter 4 to a new level and makes it possible to see everything in one place. That way, you can begin to see connections between the things you're doing (or *not* doing), and the way you're feeling.

First, there's a section for how you're feeling physically. That includes things like headaches, nausea or other tummy issues, sleepiness, and appetite. Next, it covers habits and behaviors—good and bad—that can affect your mental and physical health. (Think: servings of alcohol, hours of sleep, hours of TV, servings of caffeine, medication, minutes of exercise, hygiene, daily habits—like making your bed—and hanging out with friends.) Finally, you can enter in your moods. (The example tracker contains a range of moods: irritated, stressed, angry, sensitive, sad, focused, distracted, content, and happy. And "conflicts" is for, well, days you have conflicts with others.) Aside from helping you see what might be affecting your moods (maybe you've

Headache
Nausea
Tired
Couldn't slee
Appetite
Period

Medication
Medication
Hours sleep
Minutes ex
Minutes na
Servings c
Servings
Hours TV

Showerec
Brushed
Made b
Self-ca
Sociali

Irrita
Anxio
Stree
Angr
Sens
Sad
Con
Foc
Di

S	M	T	W	T	F	S	S	M	T	W
24	25	26	27	28	29	30	31			

T	W	T	F	S	S	M	T	W	T	F	S	S	M	T	W	T	F	S	S	M	T	W
2	3	4	5	6	7	8	9	10	11	12	13	14	15	16	17	18	19	20	21	22	23	

↑ ↑   ↓ ↓ ↓   ↑ ↑↑↑

6 7 8 10 6 5 8 7 7 6 6 3 8 9 6 7 9 6 5 5
30   25   45 30 25   40
   45   60   15 15
2 2 3 2 3 3 1 2 3 2 1 4 2 2 3 1 2 2 1 4
   2   3 2 5   2   2   6
   2 4   4 7 3

been drinking too much or sleeping too little or spending too much time alone), Bonior says that simply *recognizing* your emotions has a lot of value. Instead of ignoring or talking yourself out of your feelings—something that can lead to problems in the future—you're admitting that your feelings are real.

To note your moods in this tracker, you could simply color or check the box to signal "Yes, I felt this thing on this day." Alternatively, you could rate the intensity of your mood on a scale of one to five (with one meaning "kinda felt this way" and five meaning "OMG REALLY STRONGLY FELT THIS WAY"). *Or* you could utilize some kind of symbol as shorthand for "I explained more about what I was feeling on another page." Then you can expand on how you felt in either your daily spread or on a separate page that you set aside just for these notes.

"

"In the diary you find proof that in situations which today would seem unbearable, you lived, looked around and wrote down observations, that this right hand moved then as it does today, when we may be wiser because we are able to look back upon our former condition, and for that very reason have got to admit the courage of our earlier striving in which we persisted even in sheer ignorance."

—FRANZ KAFKA

"

Sleep tracker

Sleep is the foundation of all of my healthy living goals. I find it impossible to eat healthy foods or work out when I'm exhausted, and using a sleep tracker to see how I'm doing has been incredibly helpful. You can record what time you went to bed and when you woke up, make note of any naps you took, and mark how you felt the next day.

Sleep tracker — June 2017

		1	2	3	4	5	6	7	8	9	10	11	12+	Naps	Notes
T	1														
F	2														
S	3														
S	4													60min	
M	5														3 p.m. coffee
T	6														
W	7														
T	8														
F	9														
S	10														
S	11														
M	12														
T	13														
W	14														
T	15														
F	16														
S	17														
S	18														
M	19														
T	20														
W	21														
T	22														
F	23														
S	24														
S	25														
M	26														
T	27														
W	28														
T	29														
F	30														

Daily health-tracking layout

This spread is a simple and elegant way to attend to your physical and mental health on a day-to-day basis; you can do this instead of the big monthly health tracker, or in addition to it. A daily setup lets you start each day with a clean slate, so it's especially good for people who find that missing a single workout or having one unhealthy meal can make them want to give up completely.

tuesday
5-16-17

TASKS

x Go to class
x Work 12-4
· Study for exam
· Do yoga

PHYSICAL

x meds (8:30 a.m.)
- Got six hours sleep
- Hit snooze three times
- Two cups of coffee

EMOTIONAL/MENTAL

- Felt stressed/anxious sitting in traffic
- Felt guilty for skipping yoga
- Text from Alex made me happy

NOTES

47

Food diary

Only you and your healthcare provider know whether logging what you eat is right for you. (It can lead to obsessive behaviors for some people.) But if you're aiming to be more mindful of your eating habits, then this food diary layout could help support those goals. The notes section isn't about overanalyzing everything you eat; it's more about adding in emotions or additional context when appropriate (*How hungry was I? Was I stressed during the meal? Did eating make me feel worse?*) that can help you spot patterns and make it easier to nourish your body.

food tracker

FOOD	NOTES
6-6-17	
Oatmeal w/ blueberries	
Steak salad	Ate @ desk
Flaming Hot Cheetos	Stressed, tired
Fro-yo	
Popcorn + wine	
6-7-17	
Omelet w/ spinach, feta, and	
peppers	
Apple	
Black bean soup	Rushed, ate @ desk
Kettle corn	
Fro-yo	
Three beers	Work happy hour
Two slices pizza	Grabbed after happy hour

Full-year exercise log

This year-at-a-glance tracker makes it possible to visualize all your workouts for the year in one place. It's not terribly granular, but it's a fun way of seeing just how often you're moving your body and getting sweaty. You could also limit it to a particular *type* of workout, like running or yoga.

If you want to get more specific, you could use different colors to denote different types of exercise, durations, or distance covered. (In the photo, I've used blue for running and pink for yoga in the month of April.) And if you have a goal for a particular month (say, going to a particular workout class on Tuesdays and Thursdays), you could outline the days in advance, and then check the box when you complete the workout.

2017 Workouts

jan.

S	M	T	W	T	F	S
1	②	3	④	5	6	⑦
8	⑨	10	11	⑫	13	14
⑮	⑯	17	⑱	19	20	㉑
22	㉓	24	㉕	26	㉗	28
29	㉚	㉛	1	②	3	④

feb.

5	⑥	7	8	⑨	10	11
⑫	13	14	15	16	17	18
19	20	㉑	22	23	㉔	㉕
26	㉗	28	1	②	3	4

mar.

5	6	⑦	8	⑨	⑩	11
⑫	⑬	14	⑮	16	⑰	18
19	20	㉑	22	23	㉔	25
26	27	㉘	29	㉚	31	1

apr.

2	③	④	⑤	⑥	⑦	8
9	⑩	⑪	⑫	⑬	⑭	⑮
16	⑰	⑱	19	⑳	㉑	㉒
㉓	24	㉕	㉖	㉗	㉘	29
30	1	2	3	④	5	⑥

may.

7	⑧	9	10	⑪	12	⑬
⑭	15	⑯	17	18	⑲	20
21	㉒	㉓	24	㉕	26	㉗
28	29	㉚	31	1	②	3

jun.

4	⑤	⑥	7	8	⑨	10
11	12	⑬	14	15	16	⑰
18	⑲	20	21	㉒	23	㉔
25	㉖	㉗	28	㉙	30	1

jul.

S	M	T	W	T	F	S
2	3	4	5	6	7	8
9	10	11	12	13	14	15
16	17	18	19	20	21	22
23	24	25	26	27	28	29
30	31	1	2	3	4	5

aug.

6	7	8	9	10	11	12
13	14	15	16	17	18	19
20	21	22	23	24	25	26
27	28	29	30	31	1	2

sept.

3	4	5	6	7	8	9
10	11	12	13	14	15	16
17	18	19	20	21	22	23
24	25	26	27	28	29	30

oct.

1	2	3	4	5	6	7
8	9	10	11	12	13	14
15	16	17	18	19	20	21
22	23	24	25	26	27	28
29	30	31	1	2	3	4

nov.

5	6	7	8	9	10	11
12	13	14	15	16	17	18
19	20	21	22	23	24	25
26	27	28	29	30	1	2

dec.

3	4	5	6	7	8	9
10	11	12	13	14	15	16
17	18	19	20	21	22	23
24	25	26	27	28	29	30
31						

Monthly exercise log

If you want to be able to record your workouts in greater detail, this monthly layout might be a good fit for you. It's divided into weeks and days, and you can track exactly what you did and how much time you spent doing it.

june workouts

06/04–06/10

	S	M	T	W	T	F	S
Run	4 mi			5 mi			6 mi
Cardio							
Strength	arms abs	legs	arms abs		legs		

06/11–06/17

	S	M	T	W	T	F	S
Run	2 mi		3 mi				
Cardio		30 min			45 min		45 min
Strength	full-body		full-body				

06/18–06/24

	S	M	T	W	T	F	S
Run		3 mi				3 mi	
Cardio				30 min			
Strength	arms legs		abs	arms legs		abs	

06/25–07/01

	S	M	T	W	T	F	S
Run		4 mi					3 mi
Cardio				30 min	45 min		
Strength	full-body		arms abs	legs		full-body	

155

Therapy debrief

Therapy can give you a *lot* to think about—so much, in fact, that it can be hard to remember it all in the days after the session. So Bonior suggests summarizing what you talked about, pulling out any big lessons or things you want to remember, noting anything that was difficult for you to talk about or made you feel strong emotions, and writing down any homework your therapist gave you or things you want to remember to bring up next time.

post-therapy notes

Summary	Things to remember

Tough stuff	For next session...

Rant boxes

Journaling can be great for your mental health . . . but some-times, helpful reflection can turn into harmful rumination. Bonior suggests giving yourself a limit (like a half page or full page, or, say, twenty minutes) when you're writing about things that upset you so you don't start obsessing. If you reach your limit and still want to keep writing, she suggests you switch gears and write down action steps instead of ranting further. (Think: *What can I do tomorrow to help address this?*) Your action step could even be "If I'm still upset about this tomorrow, I'll give myself another twenty minutes to write about it."

 F THIS

Jan. 5, 2017

Is Mercury retrograde? Literally what is happening? On my sh*t list today:

- Sam, who destroyed my apartment
- Public transportation
- My uncle, who keeps posting aggressive memes on Facebook
- Casey, who still owes me $30, and who I think is avoiding me
- My nosy freaking neighbor

CHAPTER 9

List Ideas

While I love elaborate and clever dot journal spreads, I return to good, old-fashioned lists in my dot journal again and again. They just serve so many purposes! They are efficient and practical. They are easy to create and to read. They are a great place to start if you have writer's block. And I'm currently employed by a company that basically turned lists into a global, multimillion-dollar business, so they will always have a special place in my heart.

I usually have a handful of lists in the first few pages of my journal, just after the future-planning section. But the great thing about dot journaling is that you can start a new list whenever you feel like it, and then add to it accordingly. For example, midway through my last journal, I started a running list of things to talk about with my manager at our weekly check-in meeting, so I don't forget anything important. If he gives me an action item or something to follow up on during our meeting, I add that to the list, too. I later ran out of space on the page where I started the list, so I just started a new version of it several pages later, where I currently was in my journal by that point. (And because I added all the page numbers to my index, I never felt lost.)

In terms of the design, lists can be super simple . . . or they can be artistic and creative and not in standard list format at all. *Or you can do what I typically do*, which is write the title of my list in pretty cursive or a different size/color, and/or add a strip of washi tape somewhere on the page. For whatever reason, this fools everyone into thinking I'm some kind of creative genius. It's kind of like how "plain" women in movies can take off their glasses and brown cardigan and suddenly everyone who has known them for years is like, "WHOA, LOOK AT THE HOT GIRL!"

To-don't list

In a notebook that's mostly devoted to to-do lists, I think there's real value in creating a to-don't list. A to-don't list is a way to remind yourself of the things you stand for and the things you stand against. It's helpful if you're working toward a goal or trying to break bad habits, and it provides a clear snapshot of who you are and what you care about at a given moment in time.

to don'ts

- Don't stay up all night looking at dumb stuff on the Internet and then wonder why you can't get up / feel so tired the next day
- Don't put yourself down
- Don't stay silent when you witness something bad / unjust happening
- Don't automatically assume the worst about people
- Don't be afraid to ask for what you need
- Don't look for magical unicorns to fix your problems; just do the work, even when it's hard
- Don't compare your life to the lives of people on the Internet
- Don't let "sorry" become every other word you say
- Don't waste your time arguing with people who you know aren't operating in good faith
- Don't lie
- Don't wear uncomfortable shoes

Gratitude list

Many dot journalers keep gratitude lists in their notebooks, and for good reason—experts say that reminding yourself of all the things you have can make you feel more content. One incredibly simple way to do it is to list all the dates for the month down the side of the page, and then write at least one thing you're grateful for every night.

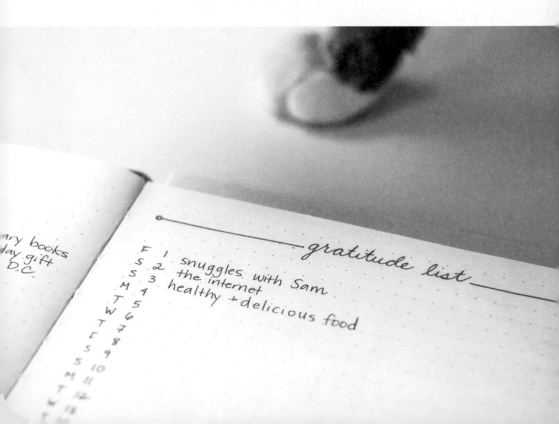

New word list

When I come across an unfamiliar word as I'm reading, I always stop and look it up. But I've noticed that it usually takes my looking it up two or three times before I actually commit the word to memory. So writing new words down for easy reference both helps me learn them and is a neat page to be able to look back on at the end of the year. And if you find yourself panicking whenever you have to say words like "archipelago" or "chagrin" in public, you could also make a list of pronunciations you want to remember.

new words
- garrulous: given to prosy, rambling, or tedious loquacity; pointlessly annoying or talkative
- vertiginous: inclined to frequent and often pointless change
- capacious: containing or capable of containing a great deal
- bonhomie: good-natured, easy friendliness (pronunciation: bon-uh-mee)
- malfeasance: wrongdoing or misconduct, especially by a public official
- malapropism: the usually unintentionally humorous misuse or distortion of a word or phrase, especially the use of a word sounding somewhat like the one intended but ludicrously wrong in the context
— slushy mud or snow — more tolerable

Shopping list

Shopping lists are a natural fit for a dot journal. While I'll cover grocery lists in more detail later, I find it helpful to keep a running list of items I need to buy the next time I go to the stores I visit the most, or—more realistically—the next time I decide to abuse my Amazon Prime account.

stuff to buy

Drugstore

x bleach
x batteries
x trash bags
x hand soap
x cotton balls
/ toothpaste
x hydrocortisone
· envelopes
· stamps

Amazon

· drying rack
x wood glue
x shower curtain
x shower curtain liner
· mop pads
· votives
· binder clips
· new water bottle

When I have money

· vacuum
· cold brew coffee maker
· smart plugs
· new slippers
· clear glass teapot

Book list

I've been a huge bookworm my entire life, and every single one of my dot journals has contained a "books I read this year" list. When I start a new book, I add it to the list, and then I go back and add in the date I finished it once I'm done. Alternatively, you could create a list of all the books you'd *like* to read, which is what a lot of dot journalers do, and what is shown in the photo here.

Reading list

- Station Eleven
- Liar, Temptress, Soldier, Spy
- x The Underground Railroad
- The Vacationers
- A People's History of the United States
- In the Country: Stories
- The Warmth of Other Suns
- x Fun Home
- x Why Not Me?
- x Tiny Beautiful Things
- My Brilliant Friend
- x The N

Reading progress tracker

If it takes you a while to finish books, you could create a spread like this to visualize your progress on each one. This is also an excellent option if you need to read multiple books at once for school.

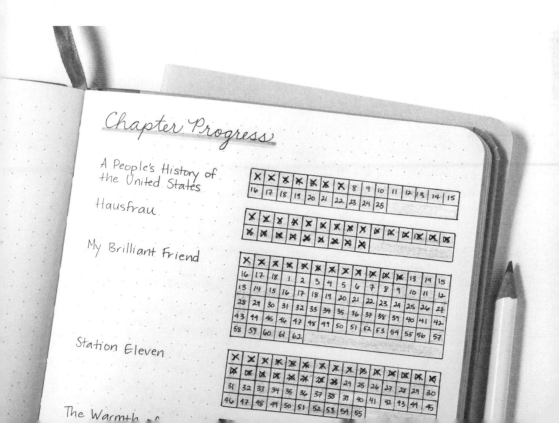

A BRIEF HISTORY OF COMMONPLACE BOOKS, AKA DOT JOURNALS OF YORE

During the Renaissance and early modern period, a type of journal known as a "commonplace book" became popular with students, scholars, and reading enthusiasts. According to the Harvard University Library, "a commonplace book contains a collection of significant or well-known passages that have been copied and organized in some way, often under topical or thematic headings, in order to serve as a memory aid or reference for the compiler. Commonplace books serve as a means of storing information, so that it may be retrieved and used by the compiler, often in his or her own work."

The commonplace book originated in the fourteenth century, when it was known as a *zibaldone*, which is Italian for "a heap of things." It helped to organize the massive amount of information that the printing press had unleashed on society. People used their commonplace books to collect writings on various topics, including religion, philosophy, law, science, and love. While some people literally cut out passages from the books they were reading (*quelle horreur!*) and then pasted them into their commonplace books, rewriting everything in your commonplace book was seen as the ideal. Keeping a commonplace book was taught and sometimes even required at both Harvard and Oxford Universities. Philosopher John Locke believed so strongly in the value of commonplace books that he actually published *A New Method of Making Common-Place Books* in 1706. Among other things, it included Locke's (*incredibly* detailed) method for creating an index to organize a commonplace book. Sound familiar?

Anyway, you now have permission to start referring to your dot journal as your "heap of things," and also to bring up commonplace books and John Locke if ever anyone tries to act like your dot journal is silly or a waste of time.

TV series tracker

Watching TV has become such a big part of our culture in the past few years, so devoting a spread to it actually makes a lot of sense! It's also legitimately helpful, particularly for shows you may stop and restart periodically, or series with a lot of episodes that can start to feel similar after a while. For example, I stopped bingeing *Parks and Recreation* two years ago, but then I sort of unintentionally caught a few episodes from a later season, and now I actually have no idea where I left off. Having a record of all the episodes I've seen would be wonderful.

entertainment

Planet Earth   ✕ ✕ ✕ ✕ ✕ ✕ ✕ ✕ ✕ ✕ ✕

Planet Earth Ⅱ   ✕ ✕ 3 4 5 6 7

Black Mirror   ✕ ✕ ✕ | 1 2 ✕ ✕ | ✕ ✕ 3 ✕ 5 6

Jane the Virgin

1	2	3	4	5	6	7	8	9	10	11	12	13	14	15	16
17	18	19	20	21	22	23	24	25	26	27	28	29	30	31	32
33	34	35	36	37	38	39	40	41	42	43	44	45	46	47	48
49	50	51	52	53	54	55	56	57	58	59	60	61	62	63	64
65	66

You're the Worst

✕ ✕ ✕ ✕ ✕ ✕ ✕ ✕ ✕ ✕ | 11 12 13 14 15 16
17 18 19 20 21 22 23 | 24 25 26 27 28 29 30 31 32
33 34 35 36

Beauty/hygiene routine

I put this type of list firmly in the "time capsule" category—it's not *not* useful now, but it's mostly worth adding because it will be fun to look back on in the future. Think about it: When you're flipping through an old photo album or yearbook, what's the thing you notice the most? The hairstyles, eyebrows (or, in the case of men, beards and mustaches), makeup, and clothing. So writing down how often you wash your hair, shower, shave, along with how much time you spend on these activities and what products you use, is just a fun little treat for Future You.

Beauty Routine

cleansing/glowing up

- Garnier micellar water (AM+PM)
- Glossier Milky Jelly or Cetaphil (PM)
- dry brush before shower (PM)
- coconut oil after shower
- Crest Complete + Scope toothpaste (AM+PM)
- Cocofloss (PM)
- sleep mask (always)

maybe she's born with it, but I'm not

- concealer (Bye Bye Undereye, tan)
- eye shadow (Memebox)
- eyeliner (Maybelline Define-a-Line, brownish black; also use to fill in brows)
- mascara (Doucce Punk Volumizer)
- blush (e.l.f. rose royal)
- Hourglass Ambient Lighting Powder (dim light)
- lipstain (Cover Girl Outlast #621)
- fragrance: Jo Malone Wood Sage + Sea Salt or Ralph Lauren Romance
- entire routine: 10-12 minutes

feeling fancy/feeling low

- eyelash primer (L'Oreal Voluminous Lash) + curl lashes
- Dr. G. Brightening Peeling Gel (every few weeks)
- Goodal waterfull sheet mask (after Dr. G. peel)
- Nuxe body oil (special occasions)
- gel manicure

Quotes

Some people are quote people—they collect inspirational quotes like you might collect plastic bags full of other plastic bags under the sink, and need no explanation for why they should make space for them in their dot journal. Other people are not quote people; they think quotes are sort of cheesy or useless . . . until they find that one perfect quote that totally speaks to their heart, helps them see the world differently, or gets them through a difficult time. (I actually fall into the latter category.) All that to say: Quotes are for everyone, even you, extremely cynical person reading this and shaking your head.

When you first start your journal, you may want to set aside a few pages where you can list new quotes as you come across them. You could also just add them to your daily spreads, *or* write each one on a fresh page that is for that quote, and that quote alone. My first dot journal of 2017 opens with a quote from the Mary Oliver poem "Invitation." And one of my favorite pages from my 2016 journals is the page where I wrote out my favorite lines from the poems of Warsan Shire— aka the woman whose poems were an essential part of Beyoncé's *Lemonade* album. The list was both a great reference to have after I returned Shire's book to the library, *and* it represented the impact that *Lemonade* and Shire's poetry had on me personally. (I swear I'm not a quote person, though!!!)

"I know, and I speak from experience, that even in the midst of darkness, it is possible to create light and share warmth with one another; that even on the edge of the abyss, it is possible to dream exalted dreams of compassion; that it is possible to be free and strengthen the ideals of freedom, even within prison walls; that even in exile, friendship becomes an anchor."

— Elie Wiesel

my pen has power.

— Shonda Rhimes

Above all else, guard your heart, for everything you do flows from it.

— Proverbs 4:23

Wins

When I started my very first dot journal, I set up a page with the header "2016 Big Wins." My intention was to add all of my, well . . . big wins. But "big" seemed like an awfully high bar, so I didn't actually add to the list very often. At the end of the year, I decided that my last journal entry for 2016 would be a fresh page with *all* of my wins from the past twelve months, regardless of whether they had made my original "Big Wins" list. So on New Year's Eve—the absolute worst holiday if you ask me, a night where basically anything sounds better than leaving the house—I sat down with all my journals from 2016 and started paging through them, hunting for wins, big or small. (By the way, marking events in my diary entries with different symbols/colors turned out to be incredibly helpful for this task.)

As you may recall, 2016 was a garbage year (although calling it that honestly feels a bit unfair to garbage), so I didn't expect to find much. But I ended up filling *four pages* with all the good things that happened to me in 2016. Some were small (I got a Brooklyn library card!), some were major (hi, hello, I sold a book!), some were sort of silly (I finally overcame my fear of using bleach when doing laundry!), and some were a little bit of everything (I found an awesome dentist!). Taken together, they made me feel happy, loved, proud, and hopeful. It was a perfect way to spend New Year's Eve and was truly the

Wins

- Jules + Quinn came to visit
- Was named Employee of the Month in Feb.
- Got a GREAT haircut
- Bought the perfect gingham shirt
- Learned to make grandma's banana pudding
- Finally bought new underwear
- Made a Tinder profile
- Got book signed by Colson Whitehead
- Learned to sew on a button
- RSVPd "no" to wedding I didn't want to go to
- RSVPd "yes" to Taylor + Tyler's wedding !!!
- Hit $500 in my savings account
- Deleted Tinder profile
- Met Alex's parents
- Called my congresswoman
- Rhode Island trip
- New job + great health insurance
- Management had puppies brought into office !!!
- Tried right-angle socks + loved them!
- Politely declined retreat leadership role
- Cleaned my baseboards
- Survived hot yoga class
- Survived dinner w/ extended family
- Got Botanic Garden membership
- Attended class reunion + it was so fun
- Did the rap part of "Guns + Ships" perfectly
- Alex and I made it through Ikea and didn't break up

best case for keeping a dot journal that I can offer. Every single entry I made in 2016 felt like a gift from Past Me to Future Me.

I'm genuinely looking forward to doing this again on December 31, 2017, and now I'm making an effort to add more of the small wins to the "2017 Wins" list I've got going for this year. P.S. While making a list for all your wins is awesome, you can (and should!) do lists for other types of wins, too: creative wins, financial wins, health or fitness wins, career wins, etc. Most people don't spend nearly enough time celebrating the crap out of themselves. Why not do your part to remedy this?

CHAPTER 10

Financial Spreads

If you are the kind of person who is naturally good with money—if you have never, say, had to give yourself a pep talk before checking your bank account, and then checked it with only one eye open—you don't need me to explain why you should track your finances in your dot journal. For everyone who *isn't* good with money . . . hello! I am one of you. Or, at least, I was.

So what changed? Well, after I finally decided to stop ignoring the fact that I was struggling to manage my student loans in the hopes that it would all just work itself out (Fun fact: That's not actually how debt works!). I started writing *everything* down. All of my loans, plus the names of the different companies that managed each one; when each one was due; and my password for each of the different websites. While it felt, at times, like that Hollywood trope where someone is trying to make sense of a conspiracy via newspaper clippings and red yarn on a huge corkboard, here's the thing: Writing everything in one place was truly a turning point. It helped me take control of a stressful, overwhelming situation. Suddenly, all this debt felt . . . manageable. And it *was* manageable.

Can you achieve something similar (or just *finally* make a budget) through an app or spreadsheet? Definitely. But I've found that seeing this info in your own handwriting in a clean, lovely spread is considerably more pleasant than looking at it in electronic form.

Bill tracker for the year

If organization and productivity are part of your dot journaling goals, you might find a spread for all of your bills useful. There is room for the name of each bill, how much it is, and the date it's due each month. And if you have any bills where the amount you have to pay fluctuates, you could create separate mini trackers for each of them, like the ones shown on the bottom half of this layout.

BILL	DUE	AMT.	J	F	M	A	M	J	J	A	S	O	N	D
Mortgage	1st	$1359	×	×	×	×								
HOA dues	1st	$186	×	⊗	×	×								
Car payment	10th	$390	×	×	×	⊗								
Student loan #1	15th	$146	×	×	×	×								
Student loan #2	20th	$288	×	×	×									
Insurance	28th	$112	×	×	×									
Phone	30th	$79	×	×	×									

VISA — DUE 1st OF MONTH

J	F	M	A	M	J	J	A	S	O	N	D
$113	$120	$304	$109								
×	×	×	⊗								

CONSUMERS — DUE 28th OF MONTH

J	F	M	A	M	J	J	A	S	O	N	D
$23	$22	$23	$24								
×	×	×	×								

WATER — DUE 30th OF MONTH

J	F	M	A	M	J	J	A	S	O	N	D
$24	$22	$24									
×	×	×									

⊗ = paid late

33

Monthly budget

If you want to do the bulk of your budgeting in your dot journal, you might need something a bit more robust. This spread is divided by category and has columns for your planned budget and what you actually spent, plus room to add in unforeseen expenses. If you want to be able to go into more detail, or if your finances are particularly complicated, it may make sense for something like this to take up more than one page. You could also use this layout for just one category (like food or shopping).

monthly expenses

	DAY	ITEM	PLANNED	ACTUAL	NOTES
GROCERIES	4/2	Wk #1 groceries	$100	$104	
	4/9	Wk #2	$100	$87	coupons!!!
	4/16	Wk #3	$100	$93	
	4/23	Wk #4	$100	$97	
		TOTAL	$400	$381	
MEALS OUT	4/7	Coffee shop breakfast		$8	
	4/11	Happy hour		$14	
	4/21	Takeout		$12	
	4/29	Dinner date		$45	
		TOTAL	$50	$79	
BILLS BILLS BILLS	4/1	Rent	$950	$950	
	4/1	Cable/Internet	$80	$80	
	4/10	Gas	$60	$48	carpooled more
	4/15	Electric	$25	$30	
	4/15	Water	$25	$23	
	4/15	Credit card	$200	$200	
	4/18	Loan #1	$175	$175	
	4/30	Loan #2	$260	$260	
		TOTAL	$1775	$1766	
FUN/SHOPPING	4/5	Target		$87	
	4/8	Movies		$15	
	4/22	Zappos		$65	
		TOTAL	$150	$167	
SURPRISES					
		TOTAL	$200	$0	
			$2575	$2393	

Savings tracker

Whether you're saving up for something specific or just want to add to your general savings account, having a visual tracker of your progress can be *incredibly* motivating. You can use this layout to measure progress in any dollar amount—so a single box could represent every $5 you put away, or every $50.

$150	$300	$450	$600	$750	$900
$100	$250	$400	$550	$700	$850
$50	$200	$350	$500	$650	$800

Vacation Savings

Debt progress tracker

Debt can feel completely overwhelming and can be accompanied by a lot of shame about the situation. But making a plan for handling it and then creating a visual tracker to celebrate your progress and remind yourself that you *are* on a path to being debt-free—even if you are moving down it *very* slowly—is really powerful. (P.S. You could also use this layout to track money you're saving.)

Student Loan

$288

half-way!

★

$20,160!!!

"WHAT SHOULD I DO WITH MY JOURNALS WHEN THEY ARE FULL?"

When I was younger, I would get really excited whenever I was about to complete a diary. It felt like such a big accomplishment! (It also meant a trip to the bookstore to pick out a new journal, a choice I took very seriously and very much looked forward to.) Every time I filled a notebook, I'd sit down and read the entire thing from the beginning. Then I'd lock it in a big trunk in my bedroom with my American Girl dolls and important keepsakes, and would sort of just forget about it. Sure, I might read allllll the diaries in one sitting from time to time if the mood struck, but for the most part, I just sort of filed them away.

Twenty years later, I'm using pretty much the same approach. Whenever I fill a notebook these days, I file it away (on my bookshelf instead of in my trunk), but I skip rereading it. (It typically hasn't been *that* long since I started the journal, and what I wrote three months ago isn't terribly interesting.) I usually reach for the completed ones only if I have a very specific reason to (like I'm being called as a witness in an extremely important trial*), or if I'm feeling particularly sentimental (like one of my best friends is getting married and I want to reflect on the early days of our friendship). I admit that it's a little strange to put so much time and effort into something and then barely look at it again, but I see my

---

* This has literally never happened to me. I go back and forth on whether or not I hope it does some day.

journals more like a time capsule. They are for this moment, and then they are for some far-in-the-future moment.

So, what should you do with your journals? I'm a big fan of the set-it-and-forget-it method. (You may want to write the date range and year on the spine first, too.) If you're worried about other people seeing them, put them in something you can lock. If you're worried about flood and fire (which I am, because I'm worried about everything), look into preservation methods, or consider digitizing them (an extra step I haven't yet taken). If you enjoy rereading them, you could make that a regular ritual (on, say, your birthday or New Year's Eve).

You may be tempted, at some point or another, to destroy an old journal. I feel you, but I don't recommend it. First, the way you feel about that journal right now may change, and you could very much regret not having it in the future. Even if it hurts to reread it now, that pain will likely subside at some point. And even if it doesn't, running from your pain or trying to destroy every trace of yourself in your worst moments is *probably* not the best idea. I have a couple of journals that I'd like to burn, but instead, I just keep them way, *way* out of sight, and I've found it's pretty easy to forget about them.

When a journal is full, it has done the thing I needed it to do, and I think it should be allowed to comfortably retire. So unless your journal is actually a horcrux, I vote for keeping it around.

"

I guess in my diary I'm not afraid to be boring.
It's not my job to entertain anyone in my diary.
—DAVID SEDARIS

"

CHAPTER 11

Chore Spreads

Regardless of how you feel about doing chores, *finishing* chores is awesome. Sure, going to town on a really filthy dish or *finally* pulling everything out of your Closet of Shame so you can organize it can be satisfying . . . but not nearly as satisfying as going to your to-do list and checking off that task. And simply having undone chores on your to-do list can be extremely motivating. Sure, you might migrate the same chore day after day for a full month (or longer), but eventually, you'll do it. (Or you'll just let it go and learn to live with your messy closet.)

Here are some ideas for tracking chores in your dot journal.

Year-at-a-glance chore tracker

This spread is so practical and efficient; you can easily track multiple chores and keep everything on a single page. For the big, don't-have-to-do-them-often chores, you could color in the box of the month when you plan to do them, and then check them off once they are done. To include weekly chores, just mentally divide the square into four parts and add a dot in the corresponding quadrant (I find it's easiest to make the upper-left quadrant week 1 and then move clockwise) each time you complete the task.

2017 Chores

	1	2	3	4	5	6	7	8	9	10	11	12
Wash/change sheets	•	•	•	•	•	•						
Wash/change towels	•	•	•	•	•							
Clean tub/shower	•	•	•	•	•							
Scrub toilet	•	•		•	•							
Clean bathroom sink/surfaces	•	•	•	•	•							
Dust	•	•	•		•							
Sweep/mop/vacuum	•	•	•	•	•							
Wipe down appliances	•	•			•							
Clean out fridge	•		•	•	•							
Clean fridge interior	•		•									
Scrub kitchen sink, stove, counters	•			•	•							
Sort/trash mail + paperwork	•	•										
Dust blinds			•									
Dust ceiling fans			•									
Wash duvet			•									
Wash blankets		•										
Wash bras	•	•		•	•							
Dust/wash/vacuum furniture				•								
Clean mirrors	•	•	•	•								
Clean doorknobs			•									
Clean switchplates			•									
Wipe down baseboards			•									
Clean dishwasher	•		•									
Deep clean yoga mat												
Clean inside trash cans				•								
Rotate mattress												
Clean washer & dryer												
Organize/clean pantry & cabinets			•									
Organize/clean bathroom cabinets				•								
Organize/declutter closets												
Wash windows + sills				•								
Vacuum/sweep behind appliances	•											

112

Chore tracker by week

If you want to get more granular, this tracker is designed for chores you do at least once a week.

If you keep migrating the same task day after day in your dot journal and just can't seem to get to it, you could up the ante and start writing it in a color that you hate, or underlining it with your least favorite high-lighter. Not only does that make it harder to miss, but perhaps your desire to not have to mar your beautifully designed page with a hideous neon will be what finally motivates you to just do the damn thing.

	Laundry	Change sheets	Change towels	Bathroom tub	Bathroom sink	Clean toilet	Kitchen surfaces	Mop kitchen	Mop foyer	Dust	Sweep	Vacuum	Sort mail	Litter box	Get car washed	Take trash out	Take recycling out	Tidy house
jan. 1	X	X	X		X	X				X	X	X		X		X	X	X
8	X		X	X	X	X					X	X		X	X	X	X	X
15							X	X	X	X	X	X	X	X	X	X	X	X
22	X	X	X	X	X	X	X	X	X		X	X	X	X		X	X	X
29	X		X		X		X	X				X		X		X	X	X
feb. 5	X	X	X	X	X	X	X	X			X		X		X		X	X
12	X		X			X				X	X		X		X	X	X
19			X														
26	X	X	X		X	X				X		X		X	X	X	X
mar. 5	X				X			X	X	X	X		X	X	X	X
12	X	X	X	X	X	X	X	X		X	X	X	X		X	X	X
19	X						X	X	X		X	X	X	X
26	X		X		X	X	X		X		X	X	X	X	X
apr. 2																		
9																		
16																		
23																		
30																		
may 7																		
14																		
21																		
28																		
jun. 4																		
11																		
18																		
25																		

"When did I last . . . ?"

I love this chore tracker because it starts with a question I so often ask myself. The example in the photo shows chores that you don't do very often, but you could just as easily use it for chores you need to do weekly. (You could also use this spread for health-related chores: "When did I last get a flu shot?" "Go to the dentist?" "Have my cholesterol tested?") It's also a good option if you're prone to depression or other mental health issues that may prevent you from staying on top of your chores. Looking at this page and seeing that it's been two months since you last changed your sheets might help you recognize that you're in a low period, or encourage you to reach out to a friend and ask for support.

When did I last...

Wash/change sheets   1/7/17   1/29/17   2/5/17   2/26/17   ____

Wash duvet   2/5/17   ____   ____   ____   ____

Flip mattress   11/19/16   ____   ____   ____   ____

Purge mail/papers   12/31/16   2/4/17   ____   ____   ____

Replace toothbrush   2/11/17   ____   ____   ____   ____

Clean washer/dryer   12/31/16   ____   ____   ____   ____

Get an oil change   1/16/17   ____   ____   ____   ____

Change A/C filters   8/5/16   ____   ____   ____   ____

Basic chore schedule

I wish I could say I know off the top of my head how often I should be cleaning my dishwasher or flipping my mattress, but the truth is . . . I don't. (On the other hand, I know the biography of every single member of the Baby-Sitters Club. Brains are weird!) If you're like me, making a reference page you can look at when you're wondering if it's time to do those chores could really come in handy, especially if you're a home-owner and have to care about things like gutters and air con-ditioner filters. P.S. If you're feeling *really* fancy, you could put this spread on a left-side page, and then put the "When did I last . . . ?" spread opposite it on the right.

Chore Schedule

Weekly

- wash/change sheets
- clean tub/shower
- scrub toilet
- clean bathroom sink + surfaces
- wash + fold laundry
- dust
- sweep/vacuum/mop
- wipe down appliances
- toss expired items in fridge
- tidy entire space
- scrub kitchen sink, stove, + surfaces
- sort/declutter/toss mail + papers

Monthly

- dust blinds + ceiling fans
- clean fridge
- dust/vacuum furniture
- clean mirrors, doorknobs, + switch plates
- wipe down baseboards
- clean dishwasher
- clean microwave
- clean inside trash cans

Every 3-6 months

- rotate mattress 180° (quarterly)
- clean washer + dryer
- organize/clean pantry + kitchen cabinets
- organize/clean bathroom cabinets
- wash windows + sills
- vacuum/sweep under/behind appliances
- organize/declutter closets
- wash bra (JK, you monsters)

"

I am anxious, and it soothes me to express myself here.
It is like whispering to one's self and listening at the same time.
— MINA MURRAY in her journal in *Dracula*

"

CHAPTER 12

Meal-Planning Spreads

My feelings about meal planning, grocery shopping, and cooking change from month to month and year to year. Sometimes, I find grocery shopping fun and therapeutic, am really into trying new recipes and different styles of eating, and get a little giddy about eating vegetables. Other times, I find the whole thing incredibly tedious and exhausting, and prefer to subsist entirely on cheese quesadillas, takeout, and sad desk lunches foraged from the office snack closet. But even during those periods, the fact remains: Humans do, in fact, have to eat, and planning what we eat in advance can be a cornerstone of physical health, financial health, and general peace of mind. So whether you're feeling like a total Gwyneth or are in more of a "Ketchup counts as a vegetable, right?" place, here are some layouts to help you get the job done.

Simple meal-plan grid

Sometimes, meal planning is straightforward: You just want to write out what you're going to eat and when you're going to eat it. Whether you choose to make your grocery list and collect recipes in your dot journal or decide to do that on your phone, this layout will still work.

meals 4/10 - 4/16

	Breakfast	Lunch	Dinner	Snacks
Mon. 4/10	oatmeal	tuna sandwich minestrone	sausage, kale, + bean soup	string cheese hummus + pita
Tues. 4/11	oatmeal	leftover soup	tacos	apple + PB
Wed. 4/12	avocado toast	leftover soup	spaghetti + salad	string cheese apple
Thurs. 4/13	avocado toast	tuna sandwich minestrone	stir-fry	apple + PB popcorn
Fri. 4/14	bagel + cream cheese	gyro	pizza	Greek yogurt
Sat. 4/15	brunch out	brunch out	stir-fry leftovers	apple + PB string cheese
Sun. 4/16	eggs, bacon, + pancakes	egg salad sandwich	pot roast + potatoes	popcorn

Meal plan + grocery list

If you do want to create your shopping list in your dot journal, this is a simple and clean setup. In the grocery list, the dot means "need this" and the x means "have this"—and that x can be added as you stand in front of your fridge, or as you add the item to your cart at the grocery store. You can also use the list throughout the week to note any items you've run out of. For example, after you've run out of eggs, you could underline or draw a circle around that x; if you run out of something that's not on the list, you can just add it to the bottom. Then when you create the following week's meal plan, you can flip back to the older list to make sure you don't forget anything.

meal plan 09/04 - 09/10

mon	B	eggs + toast w/ pesto
	L	salad w/ grilled chicken
	D	roasted chicken + veggies
	S	cottage cheese + fruit
tues	B	oatmeal
	L	salad w/ grilled chicken
	D	Spaghetti Dinner
	S	popcorn, almonds
weds	B	avocado toast w/ egg
	L	black bean soup
	D	sausage + peppers + rice
	S	cottage cheese + fruit
thurs	B	oatmeal
	L	leftovers
	D	tacos
	S	veggies + hummus
fri	B	cottage cheese + fruit
	L	leftovers
	D	dinner out
	S	popcorn, nuts
sat	B	bagel + cream cheese
	L	lunch out
	D	eggs, bacon, toast, fruit
	S	veggies + hummus
sun	B	oatmeal
	L	avocado toast w/ egg
	D	pot roast + potatoes
	S	veggies + hummus

Groceries

- tri-color peppers
- Brussels sprouts
- red potatoes
- lettuce
- cucumber
- red onion
- dried cranberries
- pineapple
- strawberries
- baby carrots
- ground beef
- roast
- whole chicken
- sour cream
- shredded cheese
- sausage
- hummus
- popcorn
- bread
- tortillas
- avocados
- bacon
- chicken breasts
- nuts
- coffee
- eggs
- paper towels

One-page sticky-note method for dinners

This layout is for people who like the *idea* of a really organized meal-planning layout but who don't want to have to redraw it week after week. You simply draw the layout once, write your planned meals on sticky notes, and then swap them out for fresh notes with new meals each week. (Or, if you eat a lot of the same meals regularly, just keep reusing them.) It also means you can switch up your meals during the week without making a mess of your page.

When pulling a sticky note off the pad, most people grab the note in the lower left corner and pull it up and off at a diagonal angle . . . which inevitably leaves them with a curled-up note. Turns out, there is a simple way to avoid this problem! Simply rotate the pad so the sticky part is on the left instead of the top; then, starting at the bottom, peel the note straight up and off the pad. You'll get perfectly flat sticky notes every time!

Dinner Plans

S	roasted chicken + veggies
M	meatloaf, green beans, + potatoes
T	steak fajitas
W	spaghetti, salad, + garlic bread
T	chicken stir-fry
F	eggs, bacon, toast
S	takeout

Staples list

I am a creature of habit, and I buy many of the same grocery items every single week. If that sounds like your household, and you are sick of re-rewriting those items again and again, you could do a spread like this. On the left, write all of your staples; across the top, list every week for the next three months or so. If you don't need to buy the item this week, leave the square blank; otherwise, add a dot to signify that you need to buy it, and then mark with an x once you've grabbed it at the store.

And if you know that some things will stay constant (say, your breakfasts, lunches, snacks, milk, eggs, etc.) but you'll still have some variables (like your dinners, or items that take longer than a week to use up), try a simplified version of the sticky-note method on the opposite page. This layout has a spot for your meal plan and a spot for the list of any non-staples you need to buy this week.

MON	TUE	WED	THU	FRI	SAT	SUN
roasted chicken B. sprouts potatoes	tacos	sausage + peppers rice	BBQ chicken sandwiches green beans	spaghetti	stir-fry	pizza

02/26
03/05
03/12
03/19
03/26
04/02
04/09
04/16
04/23
04/30

Groceries — 1/15

- whole chicken
- lemons
- Brussels sprouts
- sausage
- taco seasoning
- spaghetti sauce
- beef strips
- broccoli
- sour cream
- sandwich buns
- BBQ sauce
- green beans

"UGH, MY SPREADS WILL NEVER LOOK NICE—MY HANDWRITING IS AWFUL!"

Pretty much everyone says this, because pretty much everyone, outside of calligraphers, thinks their handwriting is awful. Even me! Looking at your own handwriting too closely is like listening to a recording of your own voice. It's just *weird*.

But hating your handwriting is a silly reason not to start a dot journal. Your handwriting is *your handwriting* . . . it's as much a part of you as your fingerprints. And you're really the only one who will be seeing it, so as long as you can read it, who really cares if it's "good" or "bad"? You may also find that once you start writing in your journal regularly, your handwriting will improve a bit . . . or at least start to grow on you. On the other hand (heh), if it really bothers you, you could take a more proactive approach.

Improving Your Handwriting with Michael Sull

Michael Sull is an author, calligrapher, and one of the few master penmen living in the United States. Trained by the master penmen who came of age in America's Golden Age of Penmanship, Sull cares deeply about handwriting, which he sees as a significant part of our country's history. "Handwriting is visible language," Sull says. "It's a form of artistic expression. And if it's not legible, it's worthless."

Sull's tips:

1. **Slow down.** If you speak too fast, no one can understand you. And if you write too fast, no one will be able to read it. So. Take. Your. Time. You should be writing slowly enough that you can actually think about each letter as you're forming it. (This will also help reduce spelling errors and other mistakes.)

2. **Don't press so hard.** Maintain a light touch; you only need enough pressure to make the ink appear. Anything more than that is just going to make your hand hurt.

3. **Research what your letters should actually look like.** Yes, there is a correct way to form each letter—and it may not be the way you learned in grade school. If you want inspiration, check out the Spencerian script, the Palmer method, and the Zaner-Bloser method. While all these penmanship systems are beautiful (and can be very intimidating at first glance), they weren't actually created with the goal of looking pretty—they were *designed to make writing faster, easier, and less painful.* Following these methods can make your handwriting look better and also make it possible to write comfortably for long periods of time.

4. Retrain your hand and arm. If your hand quickly gets tired or sore when you're writing, you're probably not using proper posture or engaging the correct muscles. The correct way to sit, hold your pen, place your paper, and form letters might be at odds with everything you're used to, but retraining your body (using one of the aforementioned penmanship systems) can be a game changer.

CHAPTER 13

Travel Spreads

Travel and diaries have gone hand in hand for thousands of years. For many people, a big trip is what inspires them to start a diary. And the dot journal system really lends itself to traveling; you can plan your trip, keep track of important info, and quickly jot down thoughts and observations, without losing precious time that you'd rather be spending at a museum or on top of a mountain. I wish I'd had dot journaling when I studied abroad in college! While I did keep a diary, I would have loved to be able to use this system. Ah, well—one more reason to start planning another big trip, I suppose!

Basic planning spread

You can create this simple layout as soon as you start planning a trip. It's designed to help you keep track of the most important things: what you're going to do and where you're going to eat. (The best trips are the ones where you just sightsee on your way from one delicious food spot to the next, right?) And any time a friend or acquaintance says, "Oh you *must* do _____ on your trip!" you can make note of it here so you don't forget about it.

Charleston trip

SEE/DO

- Firefly distillery
- Fort Sumpter
- Magnolia cabin tour
- day trip to Savannah
- City Market
- Upper King Street
- Angel Oak / Johns Island
- Waterfront Park

EAT

- Poogan's Porch (fried chicken)
- Hominy Grill (biscuit + gravy, pumpkin bread, banana bread)
- Fleet Landing
- Baked
- Husk

List of best moments

If you know you won't have a ton of time for journaling during your trip, you could just make a list-like spread for jotting down the places you went, the things you ate, and any brief observations you had each day. I like this layout because it's so clean, and because it feels very doable, even if your itinerary is pretty packed.

Vermont trip ≈≈≈≈≈≈≈≈≈

July 14, 2017

- The drive was gorgeous and easy
- Listened to audiobook version of Middlesex
- Walked around downtown Burlington
- Hiked Mt. Philo
- Had pizza @ Vermont Tap House for dinner — seriously SO GOOD

July 15, 2017

- Hiked Mt. Mansfield bright & early
- Lunch @ Jericho Country Store (best sandwich of my life)
- Ate in park
- Did Ben & Jerry's factory tour

Travel journal prompts

When you're traveling, it can be hard to know what, exactly, to say about all of the amazing things you're experiencing. So if you tend to find yourself at a loss for words, pick a couple of different prompts to respond to each day.

travel writing inspiration

1. Something that surprised me today
2. Three people I interacted with today
3. Three scents I noticed today
4. Colors from today that stick out in my mind
5. One thing I learned today
6. One thing I wish I'd done differently today
7. Something a local said today
8. Best moment + worst moment of today
9. My favorite view from today
10. One animal I saw today
11. Something new I tried today
12. Today the weather was...
13. Today I wore...
14. The thing I needed most today
15. Something I drank today
16. A form of transportation I took today was...
17. Today I was uncomfortable when...
18. Today I felt most comfortable when...
19. One thing that scared me today was...

Packing list

If you travel regularly and find yourself re-creating the same packing list over and over again, it may be helpful to make a layout you can reuse for every trip you take. Essentials go on the left, and trips go across the top. Then leave a little space at the bottom of the page so you can add any one-off items that are specific to a particular trip.

packing list

	Austin 5/10	Denver 6/13	Chicago 6/19
laptop	×	×	
charger	×	×	
phone charger	×	×	
sleep mask	×	/	
Rx #1	×	×	
Rx #2	×	×	
ID	×	×	
journal	×	×	
water bottle	×	×	
pajamas	×	×	
socks	×	×	
underwear	×	×	
jeans	×	×	
leggings	×	×	
sneakers	×	×	
wash cloth		×	
body wash		×	
face wash		×	
razor	×	×	
shampoo	×	×	
conditioner			
hiking shoes	×		
hiking backpack	×		
windbreaker	×		

169

"I'M AFRAID I'M NOT GOING TO BE ABLE TO STICK WITH DOT JOURNALING!"

This concern always makes me laugh, because it implies that you have no control over whether you'll stick with it. Do you *want* to stick with it? Well, then . . . stick with it! When you think about not doing it . . . do the opposite of that!

All joking/deeply unhelpful advice aside, there *are* a couple of things that helped me stick with dot journaling, and may help you as well. First, I knew *why* I wanted to do it, something that I've found helps me stick with any new habit. Second, I planned my initial layouts with my *current* life in mind, not a fantasy version of my life where I don't spend the first hour after I get home from work mindlessly scrolling through my phone, where I always iron my clothes the night before I need to wear them, and where I never fumble with my change and receipt at the cash register.

So think about why you're starting a dot journal, how much free time you *actually* have to spend on it, what your energy levels are like both throughout the day and throughout the week, and what is most likely to motivate you (and what tends to *demotivate* you). Then come up with a plan that is designed for you at your absolute busiest/laziest.

And if you find yourself losing steam, put a little thought into *why* you've dropped the habit. Earlier this year, my coworker told me that she had fallen off the dot journaling wagon just three weeks after she started. We talked it through and figured out what her pain points were (she liked the *idea* of doing a weekly spread but didn't really enjoy it in practice, and she wasn't feeling motivated to journal at the end of a long day/commute); discussed what she really wanted to get out of it (recording her habits more than having a daily diary); and came up with a couple of practical solutions (carrying her journal with her more, a new daily layout that she found both easier and more inspiring). Problem solved!

Finally, know that if you do stop dot journaling for a little while, you can always start again, right where you left off. Even if it's been a few weeks or a few months, your journal will be there, waiting to welcome you back.

CHAPTER 14

Making Your Dot Journal Your Own

Making your dot journal look pretty (or *handsome*) isn't a requirement, but it's an aspect of dot journaling that many people (myself included) really enjoy. I've always loved the idea from Marie Kondo's *The Life-Changing Magic of Tidying Up* that the everyday objects we surround ourselves with should "spark joy," and that attitude extends to my dot journal. For my journal to spark joy, first, it needs to be functional—I want to be able to write in it, read it, and find important information in it without much effort. And, second . . . yeah, I want to like how it looks!

I think of this aspect of dot journaling the way I think of make-up. No one *needs* makeup. But your personal interest in beauty/grooming products probably falls somewhere on a spectrum. Even people who don't wear makeup might still care about, say, the soap, shampoo, and lotion they use—they want these things to function properly and smell nice. Others might feel comfortable spending ten to twenty minutes each day doing their makeup, enjoy trying new products to figure out what works best for them, and be willing to splurge a little on the items they care about. And others want to go all in with makeup . . . reading forums obsessively to learn more about different products, spending an hour putting their face on each day, dropping a ton of cash on high-end products, and treating it as a hobby and form of creative expression. And despite what some (rude!) people may think, there's nothing inherently right or wrong with any of these approaches.

So! All that to say: Whether you're a stationery geek who gets a little flushed when talking about your favorite pens and markers . . . or you just want to add a bit of washi tape here and there in your journal . . . or you simply want to find a great black pen that is easy to write with and that doesn't smear . . . it's fine. *It's all fine.* Regardless of where you land, my advice is the same: Buy items that actually work, that you can afford, that spark joy in some way, and that make you more likely to dot journal, not less. Here are some of the products I've found that do that for me.

BLACK PENS

To my mind, a good pen does the following:

- Feels good in your hand
- Allows you to write smoothly and legibly without having to press too hard
- Forms letters and lines that are easy to see from a reasonable distance
- Doesn't smear easily or bleed through the average sheet of paper.

I think clickable black gel pens are the best way to get this job done, and I like them on the finer side—0.5 mm or less, though I've noticed that pens that are much thinner than that can feel "scratchy" as they move across the page. I wrote pretty much all the black text in the layouts throughout this book with a Pilot Juice 0.38 gel pen, which is my go-to everyday pen. My runners-up are the Pilot G2 0.5 black gel pen (which I used faithfully for years, and is also the easiest of these pens to find in stores) and Muji 0.5 gel ink pens. And if you're looking for something extra fine that won't drag across the page, the Uni-ball Signo 0.28 is great.

When it comes to rollerball pens, I like the Uni-ball Deluxe Micro 0.5 and the Pilot Precise V5 RT. If ballpoint pens are more your style, my favorites are the Uni Jetstream Alpha Gel Grip 0.7 and the Uni Jetstream Standard 0.5. I also like the Zebra F-301 0.7 (my grandma's favorite pen, and what many of my old diaries are written in), though its ink is fainter than

Black gel pens

- Pilot Juice 0.38 ☐ · — ×
  The quick brown fox *jumped over the lazy dog*
- Pilot G-2 0.5 ☐ · — ×
  The quick brown fox *jumped over the lazy dog*
- Muji 0.5 ☐ · — ×
  The quick brown fox *jumped over the lazy dog*
- Pentel Ener-Gel 0.5 ☐ · — ×
  The quick brown fox *jumped over the lazy dog*
- Pilot Frixion 0.4 (erasable!) ☐ · — ×
  The quick brown fox *jumped over the lazy dog*
- Pilot Hi-Tec-C Maica 0.4 ☐ · — ×
  The quick brown fox *jumped over the lazy dog*
- Zebra Sarasa 0.3 ☐ · — ×
  The quick brown fox *jumped over the lazy dog*
- Uni-Ball Signo 0.38 ☐ · — ×
  The quick brown fox *jumped over the lazy dog*
- Uni-Ball Signo 0.28 ☐ · — ×
  The quick brown fox *jumped over the lazy dog*
- Muji 0.25 ☐ · — ×
  The quick brown fox *jumped over the lazy dog*

Black ballpoint + rollerball pens

- Uni-Ball Deluxe Micro 0.5 ☐ · — ×
  The quick brown fox jumped over the lazy dog

- Pilot Precise V5 RT ☐ · — ×
  The quick brown fox jumped over the lazy dog

- Uni Jetstream Alpha Gel Grip 0.7 ☐ · — ×
  The quick brown fox jumped over the lazy dog

- Uni Jetstream Standard 0.5 ☐ · — ×
  The quick brown fox jumped over the lazy dog

- Zebra F-301 0.7 ☐ · — ×
  The quick brown fox jumped over the lazy dog

- Bic Atlantis 0.7 ☐ · — ×
  The quick brown fox jumped over the lazy dog

- Paper Mate Inkjoy 1.0 ☐ · — ×
  The quick brown fox jumped over the lazy dog

- Pentel R.S.V.P. 0.7 ☐ · — ×
  The quick brown fox jumped over the lazy dog

many of the competitors. And although it's not my personal favorite, tons of my ballpoint-loving friends are big fans of the Pentel R.S.V.P. 0.7.

Confused about what all of these different terms mean? Don't worry, I gotchu. (Actually, my friends at JetPens gotchu, because I wasn't sure what the exact technical differences were, either, and so I asked them.)

Ballpoint pens: contain viscous oil-based ink that dries quickly and is compatible with most types of paper

Rollerball pens: contain water-based ink; they offer a smoother writing experience than ballpoint pens, but the ink takes longer to dry

Gel pens: contain ink made of pigments mixed in water-based gel; the ink is thinner than ballpoint ink but thicker than rollerball ink, so it's both smooth-flowing and quick-drying

---

COLORED PENS

If you want to use colored pens in your dot journal, there are endless options, and the "best" ones really come down to personal preference—what colors you like best, how fine of a tip you prefer, how bold and thick you want your lines to be, and what feels best when you're writing. Here are some of my favorites:

Staedtler Triplus Fineliner. These pens, which come in forty-two different colors, have a triangular-shaped barrel, which I love the feel of, and the 0.3 mm tip gives you slim, clean lines.

Stabilo Point 88. At 0.4 mm, the Stabilos' tips are a little thicker than the Staedtlers', but you'll still get pretty fine lines with them. They have a distinct hexagon-shaped barrel, and come in forty-seven different colors, including neons, neutrals, and brights.

Faber-Castell PITT Artist Pens. I recently discovered this brand at an art supply store and have since fallen in love. The "S" (0.3 mm) pens are wonderful to write with; the indanthrene blue one has already made my list of all-time favorite pens. Their 1.5 mm metallic artist pens are quite thick, so I don't use them very often, but they come in gorgeous and unique colors and are great for header text, underlining, and big quotes.

Le Pen. Le Pen pens are slim and elegant. They come in several fun colors, including neons, and at 0.3 mm are great for creating thin lines that are still bold. If you want to take extensive notes in color, Le Pen is a great choice.

Muji gel. Muji pens are widely beloved, and are another good option if you want to write a lot of text in color. They are incredibly smooth, and are available in 0.5 mm and 0.38 mm. I just wish they came in more colors!

Pigma Micron. A lot of my friends use Micron pens for both note-taking and drawing/doodling. There are several different color and size options; my favorites are the blues, browns, and greens. (But, FYI, not every color is available in every nib size.)

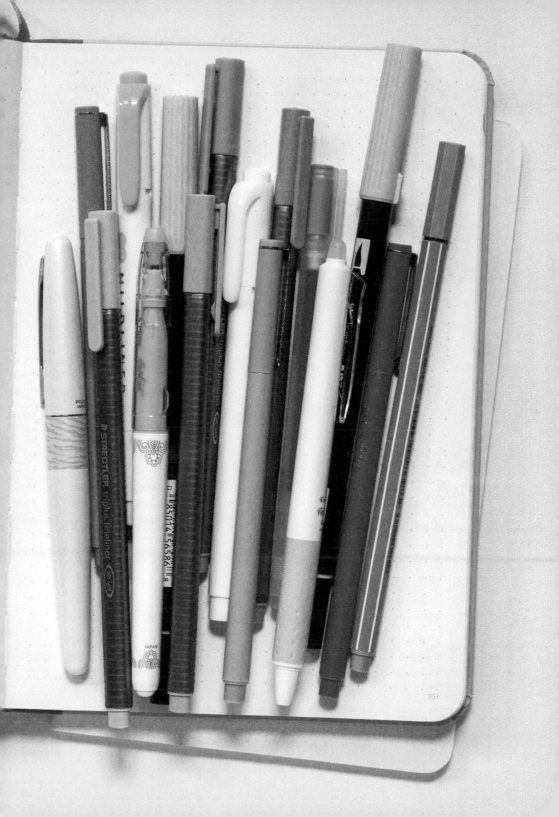

Tombow dual brush pens

942	one		two
800	one		two
850	one		two
761	one		two
491	one		two
620	one		two
603	one		two

Faber-Castell brush pens

220	notes		notes
116	notes		notes
132	notes		notes
172	notes		notes
146	notes		notes

Zebra Mildliners

Frixion

I typically only use colored pens and markers in my dot journal for items and layouts that I know I'll be creating at home (think: dates, headers, dividers, diary entries, and monthly spreads). That way, I don't have to worry that I'll forget to bring an important pen to work with me one day, thus throwing off an entire color-coded daily to-list. I don't need that kind of stress in my life.

MARKERS AND HIGHLIGHTERS

Tombow Dual Brush Pens. Everyone who knows me knows that I am obsessed with these markers, which come in ninety-six gorgeous colors. Depending on the exact color you're going for, you can either do a single swipe of color (which will give you a sheerer look) or do additional layers (for a bolder hue). Tombows are also great for coloring in large areas, and you can use the opposite, fine-tipped end to write text, draw lines, or shade in boxes. Note: These are not highlighters; if you try to use them as highlighters, your pen will smear *and* the ink will ruin the Tombows. So if you want to use them with text, you have to put the color onto the paper first, and then write over it.

Faber-Castell PITT Artist Pens brush pens. Faber-Castell's brush pens (which have a "B" on the cap) are a little thinner than the Tombows, giving you a slimmer, tidier line. They come in a wide range of lovely modern colors, so they are great for people who are looking for very specific hues. (#220 light indigo is my favorite; I use it in my dailies.)

Zebra Mildliners. Mildliners are like traditional highlighters, but the colors are much less harsh. Zebra makes both traditional fluorescent colors, and a range of non-neons. Unlike brush pens, you can use them over text (though I'd recommend letting your ink dry for about sixty seconds first). Two things you may not realize about them at first glance: (1) They are dual-ended, with a chisel tip and a fine tip, and (2) they are called *mild*liners, not *mid*liners. (I, like a lot of other people, called them by the wrong name for months.)

Pilot FriXion Light Erasable Highlighters and Markers. Today in "Whuuuutt?!" news, erasable highlighters and markers are now a thing! I had pretty low expectations for these at first—the erasable pens of my youth were . . . not great—but they actually work very well.

GRAY PENS, MARKERS, AND HIGHLIGHTERS

If you prefer muted colors or a more minimalist look, the perfect gray pen or marker can be something of a holy grail. After a lot of trial and error, I've found some great grays; you can see all of my favorites in the photo at right.

WASHI TAPE

Washi tape is a slightly transparent Japanese paper masking tape that recently became wildly popular in the United States. I like washi tape because it's a simple and clean way to add patterns and colors to your dot journal if you're not artistic, or

gray pens

Staedtler (#8)	☐ · — × > / August	mon. 03.13.17	JAN. 04 notes
Stabilo (#96)	☐ · — × > / August	mon. 03.13.17	JAN. 04 notes
Le Pen	☐ · — × > / August	mon. 03.13.17	JAN. 04 notes
Frixion	☐ · — × > / August	mon. 03.13.17	JAN. 04 notes
Stabilo (#94)	☐ · — × > / August	mon. 03.13.17	JAN. 04 notes
Staedtler (#82)	☐ · — × > / August	mon. 03.13.17	JAN. 04 notes

gray markers

Tombow (#N95)	one layer two layers
Zebra Mildliner	one layer two layers
Faber-Castell (#272)	one layer two layers
Faber-Castell (#233)	one layer two layers

if you don't have much time. While several brands now make washi tape, and you can buy it at pretty much any craft store, I'm a huge fan of MT brand tape. It's easy to peel and tear, it doesn't have a top layer of residue that will cause your pages to stick together, and you can remove or reposition it if necessary without damaging your pages. You can also write on it easily, and the color options are really lovely (and look great layered on top of each other). You can use the extra-thin MT washi tape to create colorful boxes and dividers (so no more messing with a ruler and marker) or to highlight, say, a specific week in a spread.

P.S. Empty iPhone boxes are the perfect size for storing washi tape.

One of my secrets to creating nice-looking spreads? I practice first! I have an inexpensive graph notebook that I use to test out pens, headers, text styles, colors, and layouts so I don't put anything in my journal that I end up hating. (Or that bleeds through the paper, ruining the previous page's spread.) I also typically create new spreads and headers in pencil before finalizing them in pen, just so I can be sure I like the sizing, spacing, etc. Mistakes still happen, but I like having a separate notebook where I can experiment and try new things without it costing me space in my $15 journal.

MT01P304

MT01P302

MT01P303

MT01P311

MT01P312

MT01P305

MT01P306

MT01P307

MT01P308

MT01P309

ACCESSORIES

Here are a few other accessories that I keep handy to make my life easier when I'm dot journaling:

A six-inch ruler. A mini ruler will only cost you a couple bucks and is incredibly helpful for making layouts. I prefer metal rulers because they are flat/thin enough to keep tucked inside my journal.

Binder clips. Aside from looking cool, binder clips will keep your journal lying flat and open on your desk while you work.

A good eraser. If you prefer to sketch your layouts in pencil before going over them in pen, you'll want a good eraser that doesn't tear holes in your page or leave residue behind. (P.S. If you're doing a lot of erasing, a clean, unused makeup brush is a great way to get all that eraser dust off your page.)

Correction tape. Mistakes happen; I like fixing them with correction tape (as opposed to correction fluid) because it looks cleaner and I don't have to sit around waiting for it to dry.

Brass page tabs. There are several different kinds of tabs on the market, but I love the brass ones pictured from Midori. One caveat: They can tear up your pages a little bit, so I don't use them to mark my daily or even my weekly pages—I prefer using them on pages that I'm going to reference regularly, but that aren't going to change very often.

Sticky notes. There are so many ways to use sticky notes in your dot journal; I especially like them for quotes, and to write down thoughts (or dreams) that I want to remember to add to my diary section at night. While I prefer simple muted colors

(Post-it's Helsinki and Bali collections are my favorites), you can find loads of colors, patterns, and shapes online. MochiThings, JetPens, and Kawaii Pen Shop are all great places to start.

Book darts. For a while, I was using multiple bookmarks throughout my journal so I could easily flip to my monthly habit tracker, my weekly task list, and my daily spread. I tried using paper clips to mark the pages, but they were too thick, didn't stay in place, and damaged the pages. Then I found book darts, which turned out to be the perfect solution. They are whisper-thin and slide easily onto the page, but stay firmly in place. They also make it possible to mark an exact line in your journal or in a book—so they can replace paper clips, bookmarks, sticky notes, *and* highlighters. And because they won't damage your pages, you could use one to mark your daily spread without leaving a Sherman's March–esque path behind. You can buy a tin of fifty book darts for about $10.

TITLES AND DIVIDERS

I'm not very artistic, but I've found a few tricks for faking it in my dot journal. Here you can see some of my favorite ways of writing titles and dates—and, I promise, all of them are surprisingly easy to do! And that goes for the dividers, too. My favorite dividers have a straight line as their base, a style that (thanks to the dot grid and the mini ruler) is pretty much fool-proof.

mon.
04.17.17

(may
2017)

{ tues
JAN.10 }

Aug.
04

· — · — · — · — · — · — · — · — · — · — · — ·

notes _____ tasks _____ january

* * *

notes

> >
< < < < < < < < < < < < < < < < < < < < < < < <

"

What sort of diary should I like mine to be? Something loose knit and yet not slovenly, so elastic that it will embrace anything, solemn, slight or beautiful that comes into my mind. I should like it to resemble some deep old desk, or capacious hold-all, in which one flings a mass of odds and ends without looking them through. I should like to come back, after a year or two, and find that the collection had sorted itself and refined itself and coalesced, as such deposits so mysteriously do, into a mould, transparent enough to reflect the light of our life, and yet steady, tranquil compounds with the aloofness of a work of art.

—VIRGINIA WOOLF in her diary, April 20, 1919

———

Over the course of the night, we did everything.
Yup, everything.

—ME in my diary, November 22, 2003

"

RESOURCES

BIBLIOGRAPHY

Bloom, Lynn Z. "'I Write for Myself and Strangers': Private Diaries as Public Documents." In *Inscribing the Daily: Critical Essays on Women's Diaries*, edited by Suzanne L. Bunkers and Cynthia A. Huff, 23–37. Amherst: University of Massachusetts Press, 1996.

"Commonplace Books." Reading: Harvard Views of Readers, Readership, and Reading History (Open Collections Program, Harvard University Library). ocp.hul.harvard.edu/reading/commonplace.html

Culley, Margo. *A Day at a Time: The Diary Literature of American Women from 1764 to the Present.* New York: Feminist Press at the City University of New York, 1985.

Forman-Brunell, Miriam, and Jane Greer. *Girlhood in America: An Encyclopedia, Volume One.* Santa Barbara: ABC-CLIO, 2001.

Hudson, Alex. "The Secret Code of Diaries." BBC, August 29, 2008. Accessed December 20, 2016. news.bbc.co.uk/today/hi/today/newsid_7586000/7586683.stm.

Jacobs, Alan. "'Commonplace Books': The Tumblrs of an Earlier Era." *Atlantic*, January 23, 2012. Accessed January 18, 2017. theatlantic.com/technology/archive/2012/01/commonplace-books-the-tumblrs-of-an-earlier-era/251811.

Johnson, Alexandra. *A Brief History of Diaries: From Pepys to Blogs.* London: Hesperus Press, 2011.

Kearney, Mary Celeste. *Girls Make Media.* New York: Routledge, 2006.

Mallon, Thomas. *A Book of One's Own: People and Their Diaries.* New York: Ticknor & Fields, 1984.

Simons, Judy. "Invented Lives: Textuality and Power in Early Women's Diaries." In *Inscribing the Daily: Critical Essays on Women's Diaries*, edited by Suzanne L. Bunkers and Cynthia A. Huff, 252–63. Amherst: University of Massachusetts Press, 1996.

Thomas, Trudelle. "The Diary as Creative Midwife: Interviews with Three Writers." In *Inscribing the Daily: Critical Essays on Women's Diaries*, edited by Suzanne L. Bunkers and Cynthia A. Huff, 169–86. Amherst: University of Massachusetts Press, 1996.

Trubek, Anne. *The History and Uncertain Future of Handwriting*. New York: Bloomsbury, 2016.

Vogel, Carol. "Leonardo Notebook Sells for $30.8 Million." *New York Times*, November 12, 1994. Accessed December 20, 2016. nytimes .com/1994/11/12/us/leonardo-notebook-sells-for-30.8-million .html.

ACKNOWLEDGMENTS

It feels very odd to thank people for their help with a book that has not been published yet and therefore may turn out to be part of a very strange dream I've been having, but I guess I'll go ahead and do this and hope that this is, in fact, real life.

Thank you to my mom and grandma for . . . literally everything, and thank you to my dear friends Julia L., Lauren, Dallas, Jessica, Jordan, Cara, Brett, and Julia F. for your friendship, support, messages, and memes.

This book began as a little post on BuzzFeed dot com the website, and would not be possible without the unfailing encouragement of everyone who works there. I'm especially grateful for all of my work wives—Alanna, Julie, Jess, Rachel S., Rachel C., and Nicole. You have made me a better writer and better human, and you keep me from looking like a fool on the Internet, which I very much appreciate.

A special thank-you to Anna Borges for the lovely and thoughtful work she contributed to journaling for better mental health, and the aforementioned Nicole for helping me explain this concept to the BuzzFeed audience. I'd also like to thank Joan Strasbaugh and the team at The Experiment for making this book happen.

Much love to my imaginary(ish) Internet friends, especially Jessica Merchant of *How Sweet It Is*, whose blog post started the whole damn thing for me, and everyone—journaler or not—who has hung out with me online for so many years.

And, finally, to all of the boys/men who have given me so much to write about in my diaries for the past twenty years: Thank you—I truly could not have filled so many pages without you.

ABOUT THE AUTHOR

RACHEL WILKERSON MILLER is a senior lifestyle editor at BuzzFeed in New York City. Her first job after graduating from Michigan State University was at *ELLE* magazine, and her writing has appeared on the *Hairpin*, *Huffington Post*, the *Knot*, *SHAPE* magazine, and *A Practical Wedding*. She prefers not to write about herself in third person, but understands that this is how things work.

PRACTICE PAGES

As I mentioned, if you're a perfectionist who worries about making a mistake in a fresh new journal, it can be helpful to test out layouts, titles, sizing, and pens/markers in a separate journal first. With that in mind, I've included some dot-grid pages here for you to use as a workspace.